End of Life

the essential guide to caring

Mary Jordan and Judy Carole Kauffmann

With a foreword by Ciarán Devane

Hammersmith Press
London, UK

First published in 2010 by Hammersmith Press Limited
14 Greville Street, London EC1N 8SB, UK
www.hammersmithpress.co.uk

British Library Cataloguing in Publication Data: A CIP record of this book is available from the British Library.

ISBN 978-1-905140-27-5

Commissioning editor: Georgina Bentliff
Index by: Dr Claudia Kinmonth
Production by Helen Whitehorn, Pathmedia
Printed and bound by TJ International
Cover image: Sunlight streaming through tree © Corbis

CONTENTS

ACKNOWLEDGEMENT

The case stories in this book have come from many sources and not everyone wished to have their names mentioned. We would like to thank all those who have generously shared their stories and their areas of expertise with us. They have no idea how much it is appreciated.

We would like to thank: Sharon Boylett MSc, PGDip, NDN,DipN, RGN for the information and advice she gave regarding Primary Care and end of life; Avril Luchesa and Dave Sewrey for their immense help with the chapter on funerals; Erica Arnold , Pam Augier, Nancy Bank, Sara Clayton, Jean Chick from Bupa, Paula Doyle who gave us the idea of the leaf, Bryn Edwards, Tracey Farrington, Dawn Fiske (ELManagement's end-of-life coach), Ariella Flusser, Karina Fraser, Dr Shirley Holton, Rauf Jordan, Linda McEnhill (Co-ordinator of The National Network for the Palliative Care of People with Learning Disabilities), Sarah Mould from JPA, Patricia Palmer, The Regard Partnership who allowed the team in Surrey to tell Jonathan's story, and of course Ciarán Devane who so kindly wrote our foreword.

Our thanks must also go to Georgina Bentliff, our publisher, for her help and advice.

FOREWORD

Presenting a guide to managing the end of life is always valuable, but perhaps never more so than now. On the positive side, much has been achieved over the years, building on work by the pioneers of end-of-life care. Pioneers from all walks of life have shaped how we look after those who are dying. Douglas Macmillan a civil servant, founded what is now Macmillan Cancer Support; Cecily Saunders, a social worker before she became a physician, effectively created the modern British independent hospice movement; and Thelma Bates, a radiation oncologist, inspired the first NHS palliative care team. They and many others ensured that palliative and supportive care are accepted as fundamental to patient well-being. We and our loved ones benefit from many great examples of the best of care and support.

But we also have some challenges. People are still saying that care in the last months of life feels fragmented and confusing and they don't know how to reach the help that they need. They report increasing physical distress, financial hardship, fear and isolation. They need consistent information and help from professionals to manage complex symptoms in hospital and at home, and they need support to make difficult choices about treatment and care. End-of-life care must mean care for the whole person, helping that person live with their condition, retaining their autonomy as long as possible. The challenges of information, communication and coordination will increase. Social care and health care must integrate; support at home and in the community must be as effective as that in hospital; planning during the day must ensure problems 'out of hours' are anticipated.

There is much wisdom in the pages of this book. It offers practical advice in a caring way and it is hard to say any of it is more or less important than the rest. But it is important that those of us who want to improve end-of-life care understand some of the critical things which can have a disproportionately significant impact on whether someone has a good death, or not.

First, we must understand that 'treatment' and 'planning for dying' are not mutually exclusive. Today's patients may continue treatment until weeks before death with no one point when 'survivorship' ends and 'dying' begins. Accepting a patient may die is not a failure of treatment. We must support professionals to ask themselves the 'surprise question', that is: 'Would you be surprised if your patient was not alive in 6-12 months?' And if the professional would not be surprised, then it is time to support the patient to begin their thinking and planning for the end of life. It is what the patient wants and needs which is important, and beginning to think through how they want to live as they approach death is, we know, hugely important. Those of us who care for people as they approach death must help make that conversation possible so that the care articulated in the *Gold Standards Framework* is provided.

The second thing we have to achieve is to share the specialist knowledge of palliative care teams more broadly. Working with generalist nursing staff and carers, specialists can help plan for problems that might arise, and put in place the skills and knowledge, so that when problems arise they are dealt with at home or in the care home, and do not need a patient to be moved to a specialist hospice, hospital or unit. The carers who are present know what to do and have the confidence to address even quite complex matters. A related issue is that problems do not arise conveniently between nine and five, Monday to Friday. What I would like to see is that the 'Out of Hours Toolkit' is widely used so that again plans are in place to avoid problems and crises.

My third and final priority is to do with language, even culture. While those of us reading this book will cope with the language of dying, others will not. The belief that treatment is active or palliative (but never both) and that terminal care is not about living is widespread. The tragedy is that some who could live well are not helped to do so because those around them in the community 'don't do dying' and their own fears prevent them helping those who are indeed approaching the end of their lives. A better future is one in which we as a society understand living with even advanced conditions, and understand what we can do to help people approaching the end of their lives.

My hope for the future is that every person with a progressive, incurable condition should expect to receive the continuity of treatment and care they want and need with as little distress as possible, so they can face death without unnecessary fear, and continue to live their lives as long and as well as possible. The greatest asset we have, of course, is often those around us. People who love us, care for us and want the best for us. We cannot, however, necessarily expect them to be experts, or intuitively knowledgeable, any more than we ourselves can know how to do end of life 'well' without some thought and learning.

Which is where this book comes in. A few years ago when I was caring for someone approaching the end of their life, a useful, practical and of itself caringly written book would have made our voyage of discovery that bit easier. Supporting someone at the end of their life is one of the kindest and noblest things we can do as a human, and while the loss and bereavement cannot – indeed should not – be eliminated, there is great comfort in knowing that someone we loved or cared for, did indeed 'die well'.

So whether you are a professional or a family member, a friend or a carer, or just thinking and preparing things for yourself, I hope that in the pages of *End of Life - the essential guide to caring* you will find the practical advice you seek.

Ciarán Devane
Chief Executive
Macmillan Cancer Support

INTRODUCTION

The majority of us make many plans and preparations in the months preceding the beginning of life and yet when the time comes for life to end we seem to treat it as though it is a totally unexpected event and give it no preparation or thought whatsoever – almost the equivalent of wondering who we lent our suitcases to an hour before we are due to leave for the airport. Yet the majority of us at a certain point in our lives will come to acknowledge that we have a limited time span left to us for reasons that are either age related or due to an incurable illness.

There are different concepts and beliefs surrounding death. Some people are convinced that beyond this life there is nothing and death brings non-existence. Others believe that this life is part of a continuous cycle of conditioned existence and suffering. There are many who believe that there is something beyond this physical life and that the hour of death is our 'supreme and final opportunity...not an end but a beginning' (Hudlestone 1978). There are still many others who confess that they do not know – they have no firm beliefs about what happens after this life ends, although they are very willing to 'wait and see'.

This book has been written for carers, professional and non-professional, who are supporting those turning to the final chapter of their lives. It is written to give information and support so that you can help those who are approaching the end of life to prepare for their journey, wherever they believe it will lead. When we go on a journey, we say our goodbyes, cancel the papers and make sure the cat will be fed before closing the door, so it is our hope that this book will help to ensure that those at the end of life will have a tranquil mind, and will leave behind no tears of bitterness or regret; that they will have given their precious memories to someone they care for; that they will have made sure that those who have loved them and those they have loved know they were cherished; and that they have thanked each one who eased their life's path.

Caring for someone who is dying cannot help but cause us to consider our own life and our own response to the end of life. Therefore much of what is written in this book is relevant both to the person facing the end of life and to those who love, support and care for them.

If someone for whom you are caring has been told that the end of life is near they may be in shock and so may you. Often the first response to a shock is denial. This may not be a deliberate turning away from the truth. It is simply that the mind can absorb only so much at once. It is very hard to accept something so unthinkable as the promise that life is almost over. Perhaps the person who gave the first 'pre-flight warning' for the end of life journey was your doctor or your surgeon. It may, on the other hand have been someone close to you who was entrusted with conveying the news. It may be that this promise of proximity to the end of life is not a complete surprise. Your journey to this point may have been a series of 'possibilities' – the possibility that treatment would stave off the disease; the possibility that an operation would extend life; the possibility of spontaneous remission; the possibility that a miracle would happen. In the journey through these 'possibilities' there may always be the stark alternative to face – the possibility that death will occur. But there were always the two possibilities. Now there is only one and it is shocking to have to face this.

Practical actions

Some people like to face the journey to the end of life by preparing carefully. The moment life ends may be beyond human command, but many people nearing the end of their lives like to feel that they will have a measure of control over the manner of their death. Most people would also like to feel that their loved ones will be cared for after their passing; they will wish to spare them as much stress as they can – perhaps would like to know that their death may mean that someone else will be able to live a better life. For this reason the first chapter in this book addresses practical matters.

Practical actions, such as making a Will, writing an Advance statement or Advance directive, arranging for the care of children or pets, are not only worthwhile for the peace of mind they can give, but are also ways of preparing the mind to absorb the shock, to move on from the stage of denial and come to terms with the end of life's journey. If you are caring for someone facing the end of life, then it is you who may have to help facilitate many of the arrangements. You may need to be involved in the decision making; you may have to ask the difficult questions and, above all, it will probably be you who will have to take the difficult practical actions. Chapter 1 is meant to be explanatory and clear, to show you practical things that can be done to smooth the end-of-life path, and it will point you towards sources of help. Not everyone reading this book will need or want to do everything suggested in Chapter 1, but it will give you a start in planning and thinking about the end of life.

Reconciliation

So how does one prepare for the end of life? Nearly everyone who knows that they are approaching this feels a need to 'tidy up', to 'tie up loose ends'. Research suggests that those knowing that they face imminent death are most concerned about reconciliation with those whom they have hurt in the past or who may have hurt them, with having the 'blessing' of their family and with avoiding the possibility of dying whilst remaining unforgiven for some event in their past. When faced with the great finality of death it seems we all want to re-address unresolved conflicts or repair shattered relationships. In other words, those facing the end of their life are concerned with making peace. For these reasons this book is not only about practicalities.

If we were given a one-way ticket to the other end of the world, we would want to say goodbye to our friends and the people that we love, but we might also want to acknowledge the part that we played in some of the more unhappy and difficult times of our lives. Ideally we would be able to say at least one of the three key sentences at the end of life: 'I love you', 'I'm sorry', 'I forgive you'. Sometimes those words get no further than a brief moment played out in our fantasies; sometimes they may get past the planning and rehearsal stage but get stuck in our throats. No matter, the most important part of this is that it is a conscious decision to forgive or not to forgive rather than ignoring the possibility and hoping it doesn't raise its head at an inopportune moment when it is too late to say anything at all. In many ways it is not just for the person at the end of their life that we need to say these things but for ourselves. It is we who remain to live out the rest of our lives and reflect on the wisdom of our decision, which is why it is so important to make it a conscious choice and not a decision by default.

It often happens that the reconciliation wished for at the end of life is not with a person but with a belief or a set of beliefs. Some who have rejected religion all their lives will turn for spiritual help to established religions. Others look for justification and consolation in their absolute certainty that this life and the living of it are the most important things. Still others look for a meaning to their lives and their imminent death through worldly philosophy or in their relationships or perhaps through the legacy (not necessarily financial) which they intend to leave behind them.

If you are caring for someone at the end of life there are many ways that you can help in this process of making peace. Some people with a terminal illness will be too weak to carry out or even to contemplate the actions which may be needed to achieve any kind of reconciliation. Some will have the ability but lack the confidence or the will to take the necessary steps. All of us can carry out the difficult things we face more easily if we have someone beside us to help, to support or to guide. As a carer you may not have all the answers but you can help with the search and research. You can be a steady and listening presence. You can be a partner in the peacemaking process.

Caring for the carers

When you are the carer of someone who is near the end of life it is easy to ignore your own needs and forget your own well-being. The needs of the person you are caring for seem paramount and your own well-being takes a back seat in the urgency of giving all the love and attention that you can to them. If you are neglecting yourself you probably assume that this doesn't matter – that for the present time the person near the end of life needs your all and that there will be time to look to your own welfare later. It may even seem selfish to think about your own needs or to consider taking any time to yourself. Sometimes it becomes just a matter of survival. Just knowing that this time next year it will all look different, that there will be an end to the present pattern of the days, that all our present caring and sacrifice is 'just for the moment' can help carry us through the stress, the acute anxiety, the sleepless nights, the exhaustion and the hopelessness of the present. Frequently someone who is the main carer will carry on refusing help and rejecting any lightening of the load until they break down from utter exhaustion. There are many reasons why this happens. Perhaps as a carer you feel that only you can 'do it right' or perhaps you feel that it is your responsibility alone to carry the load. Often carers say, 'Other people manage, don't they?' as though this is the clincher when being pressured to accept help.

Carers have to understand the need to protect themselves from exhaustion, breakdown and despair. However, it is not always easy to think clearly enough to do this. It really isn't helpful for others simply to say, 'You must look after yourself.' In the chapter Caring for carers, you will find easy-to-access information on caring for your physical and emotional needs. This chapter will also tell you how to access the help you need and how to cope with the many conflicting demands made upon you when you are caring for someone at the end of life.

Whilst others may urge you to look after your own well-being and may even help you in your efforts to do so, not everyone will understand that for those who are left behind (as well as for those at the end of life) there are a multitude of questions, most of which cannot be answered. The person who is at the end of their life faces a journey into the unknown – and so do the people that they will leave behind. In the mind there may be a constant buzz of questions such as:

- What will life be like when I am alone?
- How will I manage?
- How will I feel?
- How will the world look when I am single?
- How long will it be until I can lift up my face and enjoy the warmth of the sun?
- How will I support the children?

It is not self-indulgent to take some time out to consider these questions and even find some answers.

Guilt

The chapter Caring for carers also tackles the vexed question of guilt – the guilt of the one caring and the guilt that may be felt by the person making demands on the carer. Guilt seems to be an almost universal emotion and can be very draining. It can also prevent carers from taking care of themselves. It may be possible to acknowledge the reasons for any guilt feelings; also to put the feelings on one side and deal with the immediate problems. In any case, we need to be sure that feelings of guilt do not put more pressure on the carer, leading to further anxiety and depression.

Sometimes carers may be overcome with the desire to say 'Sorry', or to convey love, but find their difficulty in expressing these emotions worse than any other practical problem. There are some very down-to-earth hints and tips on how to get over such inhibitions and release our pent-up emotions.

End of life in hospital or care homes

How often does one hear the wish, 'I want to die at home in my own bed'? It is a wish that is seldom granted. For some, death comes suddenly and they may have no warning and no input into the process. A few others – the 'lucky' ones – will indeed be enabled to die in a place of their choosing (perhaps at home, perhaps in a hospice) surrounded by those they love. But for the great majority the last days are inevitably spent in a hospital or care/nursing home.

When people talk about their experiences surrounding the death of a loved one in a hospital or home it is striking to realise how seldom they express any positive facets. It is striking and it is sad. Hospitals, of course, are traditionally places where we go in order to be cured. The whole ethos of the hospital as a place of cure or improvement in health mitigates against the suggestion of a good experience of death, since, with such an ethos, inevitably death must be equated with 'failure'. It is certain, however, that more could be done to nurture the dying, to sooth the concerned carers and to ensure that as much stress as possible is lifted at this time. Some constraints are beyond the ability of the staff to lift. Everyone is aware of the pressure on beds, on reaching targets, on infection control, particularly in an NHS hospital. The biggest complaints, however, are about uncaring staff and slapdash methods of care. There are many areas where the relatives and friends of someone who is spending their last days in hospital can help to ease any conflicts that may arise and make the time in hospital more acceptable to the dying person.

There are many excellent and well-run care and nursing homes but even in some of the best the care seems to stop at the end of life. Most care workers mean well, they enjoy the job that they do and try to look after the people in their care to the best of their ability. When someone dies it has an effect on everyone within the home. Unfortunately, the 'empty chair syndrome' seems to rule in many homes. Residents are not kept informed of the death of one of their number because 'it might upset them' or 'it might make them think about dying'. In truth, it needs to be remembered that generally speaking, the older people become, the more prepared for death they are.

Care and nursing homes could change their whole attitude to the end of life. They, above all other organisations, are uniquely placed to give to those at the end of their lives the proper acknowledgement, dignity and recognition they deserve. These places, which are often the last refuge for the final days, can give those last days meaning. They can show other residents that their lives and passing have, and will have, meaning and memories of them will resonate in the future. Above all, we recommend care and nursing homes give a proper memorial to those who have died and have several suggestions that can be carried out without any impact on budgets.

For those supporting someone whose last days will be spent in a care or nursing home, we give suggestions as to how they can help their loved ones and how they can maintain good relationships with the care or nursing-home staff.

Severe mental or cognitive impairment

If you are one of those caring for someone with severe mental or cognitive impairment (including dementia) at the end of their life you will not be surprised to find that there is very little information published about this situation. Carers of people with advanced dementia have additional stress in not knowing the prognosis of the person's illness and not being able to prepare themselves for an unpredictable life expectancy. Sometimes the fact that the person no longer recognises the carer and is unable to share important memories or conversations is an added frustration and cause of stress. There is also a horrible tendency on the part of the public at large to view the death of someone with a severe mental or physical impairment as 'for the best' and to assume that the grief of those left behind can never be as great as the grief for someone 'normal'.

Those who care for someone with severe mental or cognitive impairment want to do their best for that person and most families would like to keep the person at home as long as it is possible. Unfortunately, the time will usually (but not inevitably) come when the burden of care is too great to be borne by one person or a small family. Often those with severe mental and cognitive impairment have physical health problems as well, which may hasten the need for hospital care. In the case of dementia, the gradual loss of control over bodily functions and the failing memory for everyday abilities mean that care at home may become impossible. In such cases the move to hospital or care home is a major emotional step since the carer knows that this move signals the proximity of the end of life. Although the carer may experience relief at having the practical burden of care lifted, the guilt, doubt and grief which they may suffer can make this a very difficult time in their lives.

There are things which a carer can do to give the person for whom they have been caring reassurance and also to help themselves through this period. There are also many professional carers who wish only to do their best for those in their care and who go out of their way to give those at the end of life the very best quality of care during their final journey. In chapter 6 on caring for those who have severe mental and cognitive impairment and are at the end of life, we tell the story of how one person was given this high quality of care in a home in Surrey. The story is an inspiration to carers and is included to show what can be done and surely is being done in many other places.

Funerals

The funeral marks the final part of the life-journey. Unfortunately, most funerals are organised in a hurry and under stress whilst those who wish to 'do the right thing' are in shock. If you have had notice of your own end of life you have the opportunity (if you wish it) to state your own preferences about a funeral and to organise and even pay for the event in advance. Many people do not want to think about this occasion even if they are the kind of people who are highly organised and who have planned ahead, written their wills and said their last farewells. Many people who have no fixed religious beliefs still wish for a conventional funeral (it goes with weddings and Christmas as one of the occasions when we attend church) but there are many others who would like something different. It is not widely known that one does not have to use the services of a funeral director, nor to have a religious funeral. Do It Yourself (DIY) funerals are gaining in popularity and there are many personal touches that can be part of such an event. On the other hand funeral directors today are very flexible in their arrangements; they understand different religious and cultural needs and they have all the contacts to make the occasion pass smoothly. Chapter 5 on Funerals will guide you in whichever direction you wish to go.

Mourning

A period of mourning used to be well recognised in the western world as a time when those who were left behind should be treated with extra consideration and care. That they were in mourning could be recognised from their attire. This custom has fallen into disuse and sometimes no recognised sign of mourning (as, for example, black clothing) is worn even to the funeral. This has one detrimental effect, which is that those who are in the midst of grief are not recognised. It seems that in to-day's society one is expected to 'get back to normal' as soon as possible (perhaps to save others from embarrassment) but this is not always appropriate and can lead to misunderstanding. How, for example, am I to understand that the grumpy woman serving me in the shop is really still miserable and depressed following the death of her mother and not just bad tempered? A recognised sign of mourning is required which is publicly understood and will enable others to give that extra consideration and understanding to someone who is grieving. Our western society is inhibited; most of us do not want to go around announcing our grief nor is it considered good manners to talk about one's loss except amongst close friends and family. If, however, one is wearing a symbol of grief and mourning one can make an announcement to the world without opening one's mouth. Such a symbol could also be adopted for wear at special times such as painful anniversaries. Our suggestion is a leaf which can be worn unobtrusively in the form of a brooch or lapel pin or in any other desired way. This symbol has no religious or particular cultural significance but it can be as discreet or as bold as required. It can make a statement or it can be a discreet reminder to those coming into contact with us. It can also be a simple symbol of love and remembrance when worn on special occasions.

Grief

The journey through grief is one of life's most painful passages. You cannot escape from the journey and, although others may travel the road with you, they cannot ease the burden you carry. We experience grief in many situations. It is not widely understood that those who have been given the news that the end of life is imminent go through a grieving process before they die. Elizabeth Kübler-Ross was the first person to give the dying a voice and her first book, published in 1969, *On Death and Dying* became an international bestseller. She identified some of the signposts on grief's journey in the 1970s and recognised these signposts when she was working with people who had had a diagnosis of a terminal illness and were in fact grieving for the loss of their own lives.

In this book therefore we discuss grief which occurs both before and after death. Grief is thought to be a universal emotion and not confined to the human race. It is also a very personal emotion. No one can know what grief is like for another person. It is probably true that all of us who grieve will experience shock, denial, anger, guilt and depression. This does not mean that if we are grieving we will go through these emotions as 'stages' or that we will necessarily even recognise the emotions when we experience them. It may help to know that the anger or guilt which you are feeling is a normal reaction, but it may not. In any case, most of us would like to believe that we are individuals and that our grief is individual to us and not a 'pattern' which has to be followed before we can come to terms with the dreadful loss we feel. The death of someone with whom we had a difficult relationship is still likely to engender grief and the death of someone by suicide or through some action of which we disapprove can cause additional difficulties for those of us left behind.

Just as everyone experiences grief differently, so everyone works out their own way to come to terms with death. There are some well-known actions that can help once the period of deep mourning is over and in chapter 7 on Grief the benefits of some of these actions are explained. People who have experience of grief can sometimes help others through this difficult time but this is by no means always the case. However, there is help available for those who feel that they have no control over their grief or who feel themselves sliding into depression. This chapter pinpoints sources of help and, as with all the chapters in this book, stories of other's experiences are included for illustration purposes. (Here we would like to make a note about the stories in the book. They are all true stories and we are very grateful to those who have been ready to speak of their experiences. All the stories appear with the permission of those who supplied them but not everyone who told their experiences wished to be identified or acknowledged.)

Support

Those who know someone who is approaching the end of life will surely want to support them. It is very hard to know what to say and what not to say. It is also hard to know the best way to offer support. Should we offer to do the washing or to read to the patient? Should we be cheerful or mournful? Should we visit or keep our distance? What should we say if someone wants to tell us the arrangements they have made for their future funeral? Most of us have a feeling of powerlessness. When someone we know is suffering, our immediate reaction is to try to help stop the suffering. If this is impossible we may find it difficult to approach them at all. The 'wall of silence' and the failure to approach and offer support are the two themes which occur again and again in association with the subject of death. After someone has died the same problems may occur. We feel awkward and embarrassed to contact the bereaved. We do not know what to say. We do not know how to help.

'I've been making a list of the things they don't teach you at school. They don't teach you how to love somebody. They don't teach you how to be famous. They don't teach you how to be rich or how to be poor. They don't teach you how to walk away from someone you don't love any longer. They don't teach you how to know what's going on in someone else's mind. They don't teach you what to say to someone who's dying. They don't teach you anything worth knowing.'

Neil Gaiman

There are some things which it is better not to say. There are some easy ways to make the first approach. In chapter 8 on Support the question of what to say and what not to say is addressed thoroughly. After someone has died those who are left behind rely on their friends and family and on all those around them for support to get through this dire time in their lives. Supporting a friend or a relative through their grief is one of the most loving things you can ever do. Different kinds of support are best at different stages of grief and mourning and this chapter gives many ideas and suggestions.

Many people have to return to their jobs quite soon after the death of someone they cared for. This can be a really difficult and stressful time, although the return to work can be a great help in the effort to regain some semblance of normality. A worthwhile job can also give a great deal of support and satisfaction to someone who has lost a pivotal person in their life. Chapter 8 addresses the difficulties of returning to work and suggests ways in which work colleagues can offer help and support.

Just as the experience of grief is different for everyone so is the progress which allows us to come to terms with our loss. The journey through grief is also not completed in a set time. There is a general feeling that after 'all the anniversaries' are completed one ought to be 'over' the grief and mourning. However, many times in the months or even years after a bereavement our grief may come back to us with a shocking sense of loss and unreality. Often this experience is much harder to bear than the initial period when we were surrounded by the love and support of friends and family. This is the time when it is sometimes easier to turn for help to those professionals and organisations who understand that the grief is never put behind us entirely. The experience of grief shapes our lives as surely as the experience of birth, of love, of happiness.

Legacies and memorials

Some people are helped to come to terms with their own imminent end of life by considering what form of legacy they would like to leave behind or what form of memorial they wish for. Those who are grieving are also often determined that their loved one should live on in spirit through some kind of memorial. Memorials can take many forms. There is of course the traditional memorial service, or the written memorial. Concrete memorials in the form of buildings, statues, park benches and so on are one solid and accepted form of commemoration.

> *'I am convinced that it is not the fear of death, of our lives ending that haunts our sleep so much as the fear... that as far as the world is concerned, we might as well never have lived.'*
>
> Harold Kushner

For others who are left behind it is more important that the spirit or the deepest desires of the deceased live on and these people are likely to look at the possibility of setting up a charity, making a significant contribution to an existing charity, writing a book, even endowing a chair or arranging a bursary at a school or university. Other people want to do something active and find that in so doing they help themselves to come to terms with their loss. For these people, charity runs, fund raising and volunteering are their form of memorial to the person they have lost.

There are also many unusual forms of memorial. In fact a memorial is such a personal thing that the possibilities are limitless. Sometimes the memorial takes on a life of its own and many splendid charities and organisations have been founded on the simple notion of developing a memorial in some form.

As we said at the outset, sometimes those who know that the end of their life is near want to plan for what is to come. Sometimes too the experience of caring for someone at the end of life makes those who are caring consider their own end of life and decide to plan for this end. On page 171 we have included a pull-out list. This gives you some headings which you can use alone or with someone close to you to decide what things are important for you at the end of life. What is your favourite music? What colours make you feel good? Is there a poem or a song that seems to 'say it all'? Is there a place where you would like your ashes scattered or for your body to rest? Is there someone you would particularly like to read at the funeral ceremony and is there something you would particularly like them to read? Is there someone you really don't want attending that day or someone you particularly do? Is there something you want to be said or left out on that day? If you were the director or producer of that event – how would you want it to play out? What drink do you want served or food?

Uncertainty

It is true that for most of us 'we know not the day nor the hour' when our life will end and those who have been told that they have a terminal illness know only that their time is limited. But this does not mean that everything need be beyond our control. The end of life does not have to be chaotic and dramatic. You can plan ahead. It should be treated as a journey that you must prepare for, and you can make known to others the manner in which you would like your end-of-life journey to begin. You can also take practical steps to see that after you have gone, your wishes concerning your funeral, any memorial and your money and property are carried out.

End of Life – The Essential Guide to Caring is just that: an essential guide. It is written for anyone caring for those who are nearing the end of life, including carers in residential, nursing and care homes. It is a book you can dip into when you need some specific information. Each chapter addresses a specific subject of concern and contains its own notes on further sources of information. On the other hand, the book can be read from cover to cover when you require a global view of your situation. Very few people approach the end of life alone and, although the book is specifically aimed at carers, those who are at the end of their own life and those who choose to support them and who wish to support the carer will all find help and reassurance in these pages.

References

Roger Hudlestone OSB. *God's Will and Ours*. Catholic Truth Society 1978 (reissued 1998)

Elizabeth Kübler-Ross *On Death and Dying*. Routledge 2008 (40th anniversary edition)

CHAPTER 1

PRACTICAL ISSUES

This first chapter is about practical things – making a Will, making Advance Directives, setting up a Lasting Power of Attorney, making your wishes clear about organ/tissue donation and funeral arrangements. These are all difficult issues. Many people do not want to consider such things 'before they have to'. Some people do not want to consider these things at all, preferring to leave things to chance or 'in the hands of God'. There is no law that says you must make a Will or consider Advance Directives or make a Lasting Power of Attorney, or deal with any other of the issues set out below. But many people nearing the end of life like to feel that they will have a measure of control over the manner of their death. They also want to be sure that their loved ones will be cared for after their passing and be spared as much stress as possible. They may also like to know that their death could mean someone else living a full life after organ donation. The chapter is written from the point of view of the person who is nearing the end of life, or considering what will happen when they do, but all the information here is equally applicable if you are caring for someone in that situation.

If you are caring for someone near the end of life you may want to take the opportunity to ask them what their wishes are regarding these practical matters. Do not feel that it is a subject which you cannot raise. It is truly a kindness to help someone who wishes to address these matters and by doing so you will be empowering them at a time when they probably feel they are most powerless. It can be agonisingly difficult to discuss a Will or future funeral arrangements with a person close to you who is near to death and you may not even agree with the decisions they make in these matters. However, it is a very loving thing to do, perhaps one of the most loving things you will ever be able to do for them. Equally, you should be aware that not everyone does want to give thought to practical matters at this time. Apart from the act of making a Will (which really is important) no one should feel constrained to do any of the things discussed below unless they so choose. Some people live their lives turning a blind eye to anything and everything that they have not wanted to face and those who have lived this way are not going to change when they are faced with the greatest challenge of all – the end of life. So bringing up this subject may well be met with a blank denial or a refusal to discuss it. Others feel so overwhelmed that they simply cannot cope with more than they have to and may well say, 'I can't deal with any more right now.'

I used to go to see Margaret on my way to work; she lived off the beaten track for most of the carers so even though I was the manager of the Care Agency I took her morning care upon myself. She had bone cancer and in the very short time that I was visiting her I saw her health deteriorate very rapidly. Within a few weeks she went from opening the door to greet me to having to pass the key through her bedroom window. However, she constantly spoke about what she was going to do when she got better. She lived alone with Charlotte, her beautiful Irish setter.

I happen to be a very dedicated dog lover so after I had finished her care every day I would walk her dog. She told me the doctor had suggested that she go into the hospice to 'adjust her medication'. I had spoken to the doctor and knew that she would not come out and asked who would take care of Charlotte while she was in the hospice. She told me of a charity called The Cinnamon Trust that would take the dog for 'the two weeks that she would be away'. I timed my visit to be with her the morning that she was going to the hospice because I felt sure that when she said goodbye to Charlotte she would realise that she would never see her again. I must admit I was dreading the visit but when I turned up she greeted me with a smile telling me that the dog was going to really enjoy her two-week holiday. I waited until they came to take Charlotte; she barely had the strength to hug her but there was absolutely no sign that she was aware that this was her final farewell. She said she was looking forward to seeing me upon her return. Of course she never came out of the hospice. Oddly I heard through the neighbourhood grapevine that her dog had died the same day – and upon post-mortem they discovered a huge malignant tumour that no one had known existed.

Mental capacity

Throughout this chapter there are references to 'mental capacity' (sometimes simply called 'capacity'). The Mental Capacity Act came fully into force on 1 October 2007. It aims to protect people who cannot make some decisions for themselves. A lack of capacity could be because of dementia, a brain injury, a stroke, a learning disability or a mental health problem. The Mental Capacity Act expresses it as: 'due to an impairment of, or disturbance in, the functioning of the brain'.

The Act provides clear guidelines for carers and professionals about who can take decisions in which situations. The Act states that everyone should be treated as able to make their own decisions until it is shown that they cannot. It also aims to enable people to make their own decisions for as long as they are capable of doing so. A person's capacity to make a decision will be established at the time that a decision needs to be made. The Act also provides protection for anyone lacking capacity as it makes it a criminal offence to neglect or ill-treat a person who has this problem. Certain legal agreements can be entered into only by a person who is deemed to have capacity at the time of making these agreements. These include making a Will, making an Advance Directive and making a Lasting Power of Attorney.

Advance Statements and Advance Directives

An Advance Statement allows you to make your views known, in advance, about your preferences for medical and other treatment. It can also cover other personal lifestyle preferences. An Advance Directive allows you to state under what conditions you would like to refuse life-sustaining treatment. It is sometimes called an 'advance refusal' or an 'advance decision'. Although doctors and other medical professionals may take your views stated in any Advance Statement into account, they are not legally bound to do so if they believe that acting on your directions is not in your best interests medically.

An Advance Directive has a different standing – it is legally binding in England and Wales and is the only type of living will that is so – and if it meets certain criteria your doctors should follow your instructions.In normal circumstances we would all expect doctors to discuss medical options for treatment with us, to inform us of the expected outcome and to talk about any possible side-effects of treatment before treatment begins. This allows informed decisions to be made and consents to be obtained from the person undergoing treatment. An Advance Statement allows for circumstances which may arise when discussion is impossible and consents cannot be obtained from the relevant person. So, for example, if someone is unconscious and unable to talk to the doctor, then any Advance Statement that they may have made can be consulted so that their wishes are made known. People who are worried that they may develop dementia sometimes write an Advance Statement or an Advance Directive to ensure, whilst they still have the capacity to do so, that their wishes are known to others. People who know that they are dying may wish to make an Advance Statement or an Advance Directive so that they maintain control over the conditions of their dying.

Advance Statements

As well as medical treatment preferences, an Advance Statement might include views on domestic arrangements, information disclosure, financial arrangements, arrangements for looking after children, or pets, dietary preferences, and the preferred individual with whom medical treatment might be discussed if the person making the statement is not able to do this themselves. So, for example, a vegetarian might wish to state that they do not want to receive artificial feed if it contains animal products. Someone unable to speak might like to specify with whom they would prefer their welfare to be discussed (a particular close relative, for example). Someone dying might like to specify their desire to die at home. An Advance Statement can empower someone who feels disempowered by the prospect of imminent death. It can be immensely reassuring to state the views and wishes which you would like to be considered at the end of your life and it can make this time easier for everybody concerned by opening up a difficult subject for discussion. It can prevent decisions being made which are contrary to the views, ethics and culture of the person dying.

Sometimes people think of an Advance Statement as a 'negative' document, but making such a statement can have very positive effects. For example, a statement of your wishes can act as a safeguard to ensure that others understand what your views and wishes are. It can also offer protection from neglect, as an individual can record their wishes for life to be sustained by any reasonable means and for pain and distress relief to be given whenever required.

An Advance Statement is sometimes called a 'personal values history' or a 'living will' and it can help health professionals and family and close friends to decide what sort of treatment a person might want if for some reason they are unable to communicate their wishes. However, an Advance Statement does not bind healthcare professionals to a particular course of action and they may not carry out treatment if it conflicts with what their professional judgement feels to be necessary.

An Advance Statement must satisfy the following conditions:

- The person writing it must have mental capacity at the time of writing.
- The statement must not be written under conditions of compulsion or undue influence.
- The person writing must have been able to make informed choices resulting from careful thought and the availability of relevant information.
- The statement must be clear about the writer's intentions.

Making an Advance Statement is not the same as appointing a health and welfare attorney under a Lasting Power of Attorney nor do you need to make a Lasting Power of Attorney in order to make an Advance Statement.

Advance Directives

An Advance Directive is not the same as an Advance Statement. An Advance Directive specifically allows you to state under what conditions you choose to refuse life-sustaining treatment. So, for example, it is possible to state that you do not wish to receive artificial feeding and re-hydration if this will only prolong your life and there is no reasonable hope of recovery. It is possible to state that you refuse resuscitation in certain circumstances. If you make an Advance Directive refusing treatment then healthcare professionals are legally bound to follow it. You cannot use an Advance Directive to ask for anything that is illegal, such as euthanasia, to refuse food or drink by mouth or to refuse measures that are meant solely to maintain comfort such as providing pain relief or warmth or keeping you clean.

An Advance Directive does not allow you to state what treatment you would like, only what treatment you refuse. It must also be worded more specifically than an Advance Statement. If you want to make an Advance Directive to refuse life-sustaining treatment, it must meet certain requirements set out in the Mental Capacity Act. 'Life-sustaining treatment' is defined in the Act as treatment which, in the view of the person providing healthcare to the person concerned, is necessary to sustain their life.

There are legal requirements for a valid Advance Directive to refuse life-sustaining treatment:

- The decision must be in writing. You can ask someone else to write it down if you can't do it yourself.
- The document must be signed. You can instruct someone to sign it on your behalf in your presence if you can't do so yourself.
- The signature must be witnessed. The witness must also sign the document in your presence.
- You must include a written statement that the advance decision is to apply to the specific treatment *even if your life is at risk*.

An Advance Directive to refuse treatment must indicate exactly what type of treatment you wish to refuse and should give as much detail as possible about the circumstances under which this refusal would apply. It is not necessary to use medical terms or language as long as it is clear what treatment is to be refused and in what circumstances. An Advance Directive can be made only by someone over the age of 18 who has the mental capacity to do so. This means they must be able to understand, weigh up and retain the relevant information in order to make the decision to refuse treatment; and they are then able to communicate that decision.

Conclusion

You may wonder if there is any need to make either an Advance Statement or an Advance Directive or, indeed if there is any point in doing so. You do not have to make either and you may choose not to do so. If that is the case, doctors and other medical professionals will make the decisions that they feel to be in your best interests according to circumstances at the time. They should still take into account any evidence they may have of your wishes and they should consult with your family, friends and carers. Of course, what they decide is in your best interests may not be what you would have decided for yourself. It is also worth considering that great strain can be put on family members who are asked what they believe your wishes might have been, especially if they cannot agree amongst themselves. Many family rifts have been caused by a disagreement over critical decisions that need to be made at such a sensitive time.

You should not feel under pressure to make either an Advance Statement or an Advance Directive. Likewise, if you are caring for someone near the end of life you should not feel that they have to make any advance decisions nor put pressure on them to do so. It is entirely their decision whether they wish to make such arrangements. What everyone needs to be clear about is the consequence of making such statements, or of not making them.

It is a waste of time to make an Advance Statement or an Advance Directive if no one knows about it. It is wise to make several copies. If someone is to make decisions on your behalf, then give them a copy so that they know and understand your wishes in advance. Ask your GP to make sure that a copy is attached to your medical notes. However, bear in mind that if you are admitted to hospital the staff there may not have access to your GP notes so keep a spare copy to have attached to your hospital notes. If you are transferred to another hospital, ensure that a copy is attached to those notes also. Keep a copy for yourself as well in a safe place and make sure that your nearest and dearest know where this is. It is safest to assume that any new medical staff with whom you come in contact will not be aware of any Advance Directive you may have made so draw their attention to this. Do not assume that hospital staff will always read your medical notes before they treat you.

Making a Will

As with Advance Statements, writing a Will is an individual decision and anyone is at liberty to refrain from doing so. However, the consequences of not making one are different from the consequences of not making an Advance Statement. Many people put off writing a Will because it seems morbid or because death seems so far away, or perhaps because they believe that it will upset their close family. Many are also under the illusion that if they do not write one 'my spouse/children/ family will get everything anyway'. If you are under this impression it is important that you realise that you are wrong. If someone close to you is at the end of their life it is essential that you and they understand that if someone dies without leaving a Will ('intestate') then the law has strict criteria about where the money goes and it may not be where you, or the person you are caring for, would choose. Making a Will is not morbid and it is not a waste of time. On the contrary, it is a thoughtful thing to do and a kindness to those you leave behind. It shows that you care for them and for what will happen to them after your death. It will take pressure off your loved ones at a time of grief and stress and it means that the complicated paperwork which arises after a death is simplified as much as possible.

A Will does not have to be drawn up by a solicitor, nor does it have to be complicated to be valid. It can be written by hand or printed. It can be written on a plain sheet of paper or on a 'Will form', which can be obtained from a stationer or a website. People usually arrange to have a Will drawn up by a solicitor because they are afraid that they will not word things correctly or not be able to make their wishes clear. These are quite valid worries and if your financial affairs are at all complicated, then it really is better to use an expert to draft the document.

A Will must be signed and dated and the signature must be witnessed by two people who will not benefit from any bequests in it. An 'executor' should be appointed. This is the person who will make sure that the instructions in the Will get carried out. The executor may be a beneficiary of the Will, but if so they must not also be a witness. It is usual to ask someone if they are prepared to be an executor before you appoint them; it is a responsible and time-consuming job and not everyone will wish to take it on. Many people think that it is safest to appoint a bank or a solicitor as the executor. This is not necessarily the wisest choice unless your affairs are very complicated. Banks and solicitors will charge a fee to act as executor and this will reduce the 'estate', sometimes considerably. It may also delay the 'proving' of the Will and the dispersal of any money you leave and this may cause difficulty to those you leave behind. It is quite common, and perfectly legal, for husbands and wives to appoint each other as executor or to appoint as executor the person who is going to inherit the bulk of the estate. Sometimes people appoint more than one executor. The only thing to remember if you do this is that it may make applying for probate take a little longer as both executors' signatures will be required on all paperwork (although the probate office will allow one executor to 'opt out' if they wish).

You do not have to show the Will to anyone in your family or to your friends, even if they are going to inherit under its terms. Some people lodge their Will with a bank or a solicitor for safe-keeping. Others just store it with other important documents in the home. Once you have made a Will, keep it safe and make sure that your family and those who care for you know where it is stored. It is worth making some photocopies if you like but the original will be needed to apply for probate.

Power of Attorney

Towards the end of your life there may come a time when you need someone else to manage your property, your financial affairs, or your personal welfare. Since November 2007 it has become possible to appoint someone to do all or any of these things on your behalf. You can do this by making a Lasting Power of Attorney (LPA). Prior to November 2007 it was only possible to appoint someone to manage your financial affairs using an Enduring Power of Attorney. If you completed an Enduring Power of Attorney in the past it is still valid with respect to your financial affairs and you do not need to make a Lasting Power of Attorney unless you now wish to give someone the right to manage your personal (as opposed to financial) affairs.

A Lasting Power of Attorney is a legal document. It allows you to appoint someone whom you trust as an 'attorney' to make decisions on your behalf. It can be drawn up at any time provided you have capacity (see earlier) but has no legal standing until it is registered with the Office of the Public Guardian. The rules for an Enduring Power of Attorney are different and you can find out about this by contacting the Office of the Public Guardian or checking the Office's website.

You can create two types of LPA and there is an important difference concerning when each can be used in respect of mental capacity.

Property and Affairs LPA

A Property and Affairs LPA allows you (the donor) to choose someone to make decisions about how to spend your money and the way your property and affairs are managed. Once registered, a Lasting Power of Attorney for Property and Affairs can be used at any time, whether you have the mental ability to act for yourself or not. This means that if you still have capacity to manage your affairs but would rather the attorney did this for you (perhaps because you are ill) then they can do so. You can continue or resume managing your own property and financial affairs at any time. Alternatively, you, the donor, may include a restriction that the LPA can be used only at a time in the future when you lack the capacity to make decisions for yourself – for example, due to the onset of dementia in later life or as a result of a brain injury.

Personal Welfare LPA

A Personal Welfare LPA allows you to choose someone to make decisions about your healthcare and welfare. This includes making decisions to refuse or consent to treatment on your behalf and deciding where you will live. These decisions can be taken on your behalf only when the LPA has been registered and you lack the capacity to make the decisions yourself. You can appoint more than one person as attorney and some people feel safer doing so. However, it is important to remember that if you appoint two or more people to act jointly this will be likely to slow up any actions they may need to take. For example, more than one signature will be required on documents. Appointing two or more people to act jointly may also mean that the LPA is cancelled if one of the attorneys dies or loses the capacity to act. It is also possible to appoint two or more attorneys to act together and independently or to act together on certain issues and independently on others.

An LPA can contain restrictions and/or conditions that place limits on the decisions the attorney can take – for example, it can state that the attorney may only be allowed to make decisions about where the donor lives or may not be able to sell the donor's house. The attorney must adhere to these restrictions and conditions. The donor may also include guidance in his/her LPA to assist the attorney when making decisions in his/her best interests. The attorney should take account of this guidance when making decisions for the donor.

Making a Lasting Power of Attorney needs careful thought. Full guidance on this is available from the Office of the Public Guardian and online at the Office's website (see page 32).

Organ and tissue donation after death

Organ donation is the gift of an organ to help someone who needs a transplant. Kidneys, heart, liver, lungs, pancreas and the small bowel can all be transplanted. Tissue donation is the gift of tissue such as corneas, skin, bone, tendons, cartilage and heart valves. Most people can donate tissue. Unlike organs, it may be possible to donate tissue up to 48 hours after a person has died.

Reproductive organs and reproductive tissue are not taken from dead donors in the UK. In the UK, organs and tissue will be used only if a potential donor has indicated that this is his/her wish (although a change in this law is under discussion). Anyone wishing to donate organs or tissue can indicate this in a number of ways:

- Simply telling a relative or close friend is an indication of a wish to donate.
- Completing and carrying an organ donor card.
- Recording your wishes on the NHS Organ Donor Register.
- Adding your wishes to an Advance Statement.

Putting your name on the NHS Organ Donor Register makes it easier for the NHS to establish your wishes and for those closest to you to follow them.

If your wishes are not clear, the person closest to you in life will be asked what they think you would have wanted, so it is important that they are aware of your views on organ donation. It is not a good idea to rely on a statement in your Will as frequently a Will is not read until days or even weeks after a death. It will then be too late to arrange organ or tissue donation. The NHS Organ Donor Register is a confidential, computerised database that holds the wishes of people who have decided that, after their death, they want to leave a legacy of life for others by donating tissue or organs. The register is used to help establish whether a person wanted to donate and, if so, what.

Sometimes people who would otherwise like to donate organs or tissue decide not to express this wish because they are afraid that doctors and other health professionals will take less care of them (or perhaps even pronounce them dead too soon) if they know that they are a potential donor. It is important to understand that organs are removed for transplantation only after a person has died. Death is confirmed by a doctor or doctors who are entirely independent of any transplant team and death is confirmed in exactly the same way for people who donate organs as for those who do not.

Sometimes a person on a ventilator (which is theoretically keeping them 'alive') may actually be certified as dead because their brain is no longer functioning. There are very clear and strict standards and procedures for doing the tests to confirm death in these circumstances and they are always performed by two experienced doctors.

Having a medical condition does not necessarily prevent a person from becoming an organ or tissue donor. The decision about whether some or all organs or tissues are suitable for transplant will be made by a healthcare professional, taking into account the medical history of the donor. There are only two conditions where organ donation is ruled out completely. A person cannot become an organ or tissue donor if they have been diagnosed as HIV positive, or if they have, or are suspected of having, CJD (Creutzfeld Jacob's disease).

Although donating organs or tissue after your death is a selfless and generous thing to do, someone who is approaching the end of life should not feel pressurised to do this. People may have personal and ethical reasons why they do not wish to become a donor and those caring for them should respect their reasons. Sometimes people have no objection to donating but do not wish to go through the process of formally registering as a donor (perhaps because they do not wish to think about their death in advance). If you are caring for someone in this position you may wish to discuss this together so that if you are approached as next of kin following the death of your loved one you will at least know what their wishes were.

Planning a funeral in advance

Planning your funeral now may be the last thing that you want to be thinking about, but when life ends it does help to ease the emotional and financial strain on friends, family and loved ones at a very difficult time if you have made your wishes known beforehand. Some people may find that planning their funeral actually brings comfort and reassurance.

It is fairly simple to record your exact wishes and also possible to fix many of the costs by planning ahead. Many people take out funeral plans, providing them with the comfort that this need not be a burden to those they have left behind. Almost all funeral directors will be prepared to discuss such an arrangement and to show you any pre-prepared plans or schemes that they have available. However, if you do not wish to do anything as formal as this but want to make your wishes known, you could write them down and file them with your Will. Be sure to tell those closest to you that you have recorded your wishes and keep a separate copy for them as it is possible that your Will may not be opened in time to carry out your wishes concerning the funeral.

Further information about planning a funeral is available in chapter 5.

Making future arrangements for children or other dependants

If you die without making a Will, or if you do not appoint guardians to your children in your Will, your children could be placed in care until the court appoints official guardians to look after them. This could take a long time and would obviously result in distress for your children and other members of your family. Appointing guardians can safeguard against this happening. Most parents appoint relatives or friends who they think would care well for their children should they die. It is important to ask potential guardians before you name them in your Will as they must agree to accept their role and be aware of their responsibilities.

You can appoint different guardians for different children but this may mean splitting them up into different homes following your death. Guardians have to ensure adequate contact between the children is maintained, but you may not be happy having your children divided in any way.

Guardians are appointed only for children under the age of 18. An important point is to remember to request that your appointed guardians also make a Will themselves to safeguard the future of your children further.

Making decisions

The information above has been written so that anyone who needs to consider these practical matters can find out the basics quickly and easily. We have not tried to answer all possible questions but have included references and website addresses so that further information is simple to obtain.

It is not always easy to consider any of these matters. You may have little time in which to do so. You are almost certainly painfully aware that thinking about these things is difficult not only for you but for those you care for or who care for you.

You do not need to tackle the practical issues all at once, or even to tackle them at all. It might help to make your plans and carry out your preparations in small steps. Take one small step at a time. Consider what is most important for you. Maybe you will address that point only.

Perhaps you will choose to talk to someone about your, or their, wishes so that you all understand what these are. (We include an example of end of life wishes on page 171.) Perhaps you will make an appointment with a solicitor to draw up a Will. Perhaps you will consult one web page or make one telephone call. Even one small step can be immensely useful and it will help you make another small step if and when you are ready.

If you are caring for someone near the end of their life it will be painful to have to talk about their passing and about a time when they will have left you, but by discussing things as and when the person at the end of life wishes to do so, by giving them whatever help you can and by understanding their need to do these things, you are giving them the ultimate gift of your love.

Assisted suicide

There has recently been much media attention on the subject of assisted suicide. The Director of Public Prosecutions has made it clear that as the law stands, 'A person commits an offence if he or she aids, abets, counsels or procures... the suicide of another, or the attempt by another to commit suicide.' Further guidance on the subject is available in the Interim Policy for Prosecutors in Respect of Cases of Assisted Suicide (see www.cps.gov.uk).

Further sources of help and information

Office of the Public Guardian
Tel: 0845 330 2900
Website: www.publicguardian.gov.uk

Organ and tissue donation
You can find out more about organ and tissue donation at
www.uktransplant.org.uk

Leaving your body to science
If you are interested in leaving your body for medical research purposes and you live in England or Wales, you can find out more at
www.hta.gov.uk

Caring for pets
The Cinnamon Trust is the national charity for the elderly and their pets. The only specialist national charity for people in their last years and their much-loved animals.
Website: www.cinnamon.org.uk

Making a Will
Guidance on making a Will, plus information on where to get further help:
Website:www.direct.gov.uk/en/Governmentcitizensandrights/Death/ Preparation/DG_10029800

CHAPTER 2

MAKING PEACE

It is paramount that those caring for someone at the end of life recognise the holistic nature of end-of-life needs. Holistic is a word often used and rarely understood. It is rooted in the word 'holism', meaning that the sum of the parts is greater than the whole. In medicine the word holistic is generally used to describe a treatment approach which looks at the whole body rather than just the individual afflicted body part. In this book we use the word to mean that the body, mind and spirit are not independent of one another; they are intertwined and what affects one affects the others. A philosophy or treatment that focuses on only one aspect of body, mind or spirit is not only an incomplete approach, but one that will be of less benefit to the patient.

The ancients appeared to understand this connection better than we do today. Hippocrates, for example, said: 'Then we must consider the patient ... the patient's customs, mode of life, pursuits and age. Then we must consider his speech, his mannerisms, his silences, his thoughts, his habits of sleep or wakefulness and his dreams, their nature and time.'

St Benedict, writing his 'rule' in the sixth century AD, laid down that the monks in the monasteries that ascribed to his rule should give equal weight to physical work (the body), learning or teaching (the mind), and prayer and worship (the spirit). The entire monastic day and night was divided so that each of these areas received proper attention.

At the end of life, perhaps more than at any other time, we should be addressing the needs of the whole person – the mind, the body and the spirit.

Everyone reacts differently to the news that the end of life is near.

Some are violently upset, some are sad, some are perhaps philosophical. The fact is, however, that nearly everyone who knows that they are approaching the end of life feels a need to 'tidy up', to 'tie up loose ends'. For some people this need takes the form of taking practical steps to make sure that the family they leave behind will be financially secure or well looked after (making a Will, arranging guardianship of children). Others may wish to leave a legacy in the form of tissue or organ donation (see chapter 1). Some people like to plan their own funeral or memorial service (chapters 5 and 9). For some people, however, these practical matters take second place (or perhaps equal place) to the need to re-address unresolved conflicts, to rebuild a shattered relationship, to put right a wrong done in the past or in some other way to make peace both with themselves and with those connected to them.

When Gallup International Institute carried out a national survey in 1997 on 'Spiritual beliefs and the dying process', the key spiritual concerns mentioned by people questioned were:

- Not being forgiven by someone for something they had done;
- Not having a blessing from a family member or religious advisor.

When considering questions about life after death the reassurances that gave people the most comfort related to these concerns:

- Desire for reconciliation with those they had hurt, or who had hurt them; and
- The belief that death is not the end, but a passage.

There is a universal desire to leave something of ourselves behind, to leave a legacy. For some it is enough that they have children. Others search for a way to leave something behind that will be truly lasting. Those who have the necessary funds may want to leave a financial legacy for family and/or the community. Many feel that setting up a trust or donating money to an institute, or service, with a request to have that building or service named after them, will leave a lasting legacy (see chapter 9).

Recent reminiscence work in the areas of both dementia care and bereavement has centred around the idea of leaving a box filled with pictures and mementoes. These 'memory boxes' may also contain letters explaining the importance of the different objects.

Another frequently adopted memorial idea is to include letters written to children, grandchildren or even great grandchildren to be opened and read by the child at a certain age or event in the child's life. Others record a videoed-message, a spoken life history, or messages for different members of the family. Grandparents or parents who have been diagnosed with terminal illness may have a strong wish for their children or grandchildren to know more about them and consider that in this way they can be a continuous presence in their lives.

People at the end of life often feel an urgent need or desire to write their life story, perhaps reflecting a need to know that they will not be forgotten, that their life will have meaning, that they have contributed something to the world and that this contribution will be recognised and not forgotten. People want to have their life 'witnessed'. No one wants to think that their life holds no meaning for others and will be forgotten. It is easy for children to forget that their parents were once young, once loved, were once foolish, perhaps once suffered, overcame difficulties and climbed emotional mountains. Many feel that if no one knows about this past it is almost as though it never happened. The closer individuals get to the end of life the more some may feel the urgent need to have their lives and accomplishments recognised.

There are many ways of leaving a tangible legacy and this is covered in greater depth in chapter 9. Most carers understand that meeting the spiritual needs of the person at the end of their life is essential. Yet addressing these seems so much harder than dealing with physical needs. If someone is hungry we can feed them. If they are in pain we can administer pain relief. But suppose their spirit yearns for sustenance? The problem seems to arise because to each person spirituality has a different meaning. There are also problems addressing spiritual needs in a hospital setting. Although health services currently aim to cater for people's physical needs, their spiritual needs are mostly neglected or ignored. Health professionals in general are, indeed, actively discouraged from either attending to the patient's spiritual needs or revealing any spiritual beliefs that they themselves may personally hold. The World Health Organisation has a definition: 'The spiritual dimension of human life may be seen as holding together the physical, psychological and social components, is often understood as being concerned with meaning and purpose, and for those nearing the end of life, is commonly associated with the need for forgiveness, reconciliation and affirmation of worth.' (WHO 1990)

Every serious illness brings up questions. The more advanced the illness the bigger the questions asked, and the closer people are to facing the end of their life the more profound (and unanswerable) their questions become. Consider questions such as:

Why is this happening to me?

Is there life after death?

Where is God now?

What will the world look like after I'm gone?

These may be questions that cannot easily be answered, but that does not mean that they cannot be addressed. Saying, 'I wish I could answer your questions ...' is an acceptable and empathetic response if you do not feel able to go further. Sometimes it is helpful and appropriate to ask, 'What are your beliefs?' or 'What gives you comfort?' or perhaps, 'Is there anything you would find comforting now?' This may help the person at the end of life to ask for what they want or to come to their own conclusions about beliefs they have been struggling with.

My father had been a 'lapsed catholic' since the major changes to church services in the sixties. When he was seriously ill in hospital we all skirted around the religious question until one day my elder sister simply asked, 'Dad, would you like to see the priest when he comes round?' My father did see the priest and gained great comfort. I know he wouldn't have asked for himself because he would have felt he was being hypocritical after taking a stand earlier in his life.

> *My parents divorced when my brothers and I were quite young.*
> *When Mum was in her last illness one of her friends visited and*
> *asked her if there was anything which would bring her special*
> *comfort. Mum said she would like to see my Dad to say goodbye.*
> *I don't think she would have told us this because she knew we*
> *always resented Dad and believed it was his fault the divorce*
> *had taken place.*

If you are caring for someone at the end of life it may sometimes be absolutely appropriate to state your own beliefs, whilst of course emphasising that they are your personal beliefs and understanding that they are not necessarily shared. For example, if someone asks you, 'Why do you suppose God has done this to me?' it may be acceptable to say something like, 'I don't know the answer to that but I personally believe that there is a reason behind everything that happens. I believe God has a plan for each of us.' It is much less acceptable to make statements such as 'It is God's will' or 'God never gives you more than you can bear' unless you know that such statements coincide with the questioner's philosophy.

Those people who have a strong religious belief can find this a great comfort at the end of life. But for some this belief may make their last days more anxious, particularly if they feel guilt or anger at something which has happened in the past and they believe that after death they will have to answer for this. If someone expresses their beliefs about life after death, then it would be quite inappropriate for anyone caring for them to argue about this, even if their own beliefs do not coincide. If the person who is at the end of life is serene and comfortable with the belief that they are going to pass on into an afterlife (for example, they may express the belief that they will meet up with a loved one who has died) then, as a carer, you have nothing to do but concur gracefully or if you feel unable to do so you can confine your replies to such statements as:

'I am so glad you feel that way.'

'That must be very comforting.'

If, however, the person for whom you are caring is anxious and depressed because of their beliefs, then it is best to arrange for them to talk to a minister of their own religion who will feel better able to answer any questions or give consolation or absolution. It is not easy to start a conversation and talk about spiritual matters with someone who is dying. We can know someone for a long time – even quite intimately – but never have discussed spiritual matters with them. If you know or feel that it is an important area to address, or you have concerns about their spiritual state, some of these questions may be helpful to open up the conversation:

'Are you a religious or spiritual person?'

'What gives meaning to your life?'

'What does spirituality mean to you? Is it important to you?'

'Do you have worries or fears regarding spirituality or religion?'

'How can I/we help you to get spiritual care?'

'Would you like to see a chaplain, rabbi, priest or is there anyone you would like to see and talk to?'

There are undoubtedly times when it is appropriate to ask this last question, but there is a need to be sensitive to the feelings behind questions put to you. Someone asking, 'What is going to happen?' may be trying to lead into a discussion on a possible afterlife or may simply want to know their own prognosis. Sometimes people just want to talk about their illness and to know more about what physical symptoms to expect. They may feel that being more prepared and knowing what to expect can give them the strength to prepare. There are many connections between the physical body and the emotions. No matter how physically comfortable someone is when they are close to the end of their life, if they have pressing matters on their mind they will be deeply uncomfortable and restless.

People at the end of life often feel the need to reconnect with lost family or those who were once close friends. Whenever it is at all possible, it is a wonderful gift to try and make achievable dreams come true. With the help of the internet and social networking sites it is easier than ever to find a way to reconnect with lost associations. Sometimes just a telephone call from a relative who has long been out of touch may make the person at the end of life feel as if they have 'reconnected'. Elderly people often get great joy from seeing grandchildren during their final days. Perhaps they get comfort from the thought that their 'line' is being continued down the generations. Often parents and others feel that young children will be frightened at seeing Granny or Grandad in hospital, perhaps will become upset at the sight of medical equipment (such as oxygen masks) in use. Actually children are very matter of fact about things which may upset adults. Partly this is because they do not understand the implications of drip tubes, breathing apparatus and so on. Partly it is because children seem to have a natural ability to 'screen out' things which might otherwise disturb them. Children who are old enough to understand can be given simple answers to questions ('Granny finds it hard to breathe and the tube helps her'), but often even this is not necessary. Most children will understand that 'it makes Grandad very happy to see you' without any further explanation being necessary.

My mum didn't actually ask each of us to come and see her during her last days. She was very undemanding and wouldn't have thought it right to ask such a 'favour' herself. However, all my brothers and sisters came to the hospital over the last few days, some of us travelling a great distance to see Mum. She didn't say anything directly to thank us but the day before she died I remember her saying quietly to me, 'I've seen everyone now,' as though she had fulfilled some promise to herself.

Most people who know that their life is coming to an end will begin to think about how they have spent the time they have had. This is a time when someone weighs up their past actions, their accomplishments and failures and tries to make a balance. They may ask themselves, 'Have I been a good person, parent, sibling, child?' This 'balancing' can lead to a need or a wish to confess or to atone and to try to come to terms with issues from the past or, as discussed above, to re-connect to roots or community. This can also be a time when regrets and guilt come to the fore – it can be a very challenging time for someone who feels that they have lived an unfulfilled life. They need to come to terms with the loss of hope and dreams.

At the end of life many have to wrestle with feelings of guilt. Visions of past 'failures' may haunt the last days. Some may rehearse over and over again all the things that could have been done differently ... 'if only'. Guilt may combine with anger. There may be a feeling that the end of life would not be approaching if 'someone' had done or not done something. Guilt may result in bargaining: 'If only I do not die I will make it up with so and so.' The person at the end of life may get very depressed and spend hours trying to work out where 'it all went wrong'. Guilt is a normal emotion to experience when grieving and someone who knows they are at the end of life (particularly if it is felt that life is ending 'prematurely') is likely to grieve for the life they would have had.

My mother died prematurely, at 48. She was taken ill very suddenly and we only had a few days to prepare. We all took it in turns to sit by her bedside over a period of three days; she was never left by herself. Interestingly it was when my sister-in-law was alone with her that my mother felt safe to tell her that she had had a child, a boy, 'out of wedlock' when she was 17 that she had been forced to give up for adoption – a decision she had regretted every day for 31 years. She asked my sister-in-law to tell the family after she had died because she felt she couldn't bear to – and asked her to make sure the family did whatever they could to trace him and ask his forgiveness on her behalf. She gave her all the details and made her swear not to speak about this until after the funeral. My mother died that night. I wondered if once she had told someone that secret she felt more prepared to die.

This can be a very challenging time for the carer and for all the friends, relatives and contacts of the person whose end of life is near. Of course there is a natural urge to 'fix' things, to think that even if you can't save the life which is ebbing away perhaps you can make the passing easier. You can bring lost relatives across the world, you can try to reconcile those at odds with each other, you can surround the dying person with all the things they like best, the food they enjoy, the music they love, the people they would most like to see.

It is true that maybe you can do all or any of these things, but you can also do something which may be much harder to do and yet more valuable. You can listen. You can give freely of your time and energy to sit and listen without judgement, without trying to find clichés to fill the silences. You can just allow the person to voice their thoughts. There may be no need to make specific responses. It can sometimes help to encourage someone voicing their thoughts and concerns if you ask quiet leading questions, such as: 'How do you feel about that now?' or, 'Do you feel you should have done more?' Equally, it may be just as appropriate to say nothing or to make some neutral response such as: 'Yes. I remember.' Sometimes just saying, 'I am here. You are not alone,' is enough to bring comfort.

> *My mother-in-law was dying and I was the only family member who could be with her at the end. I had had a fairly standard mother/daughter-in-law relationship and I am sure she wished her son was with her but he was stranded abroad. I really hadn't a clue what to say or do so I just held her hand and when she opened her eyes or stirred I said, 'It's all right, Muriel. I'm here with you. Steven is coming soon.' I know she could hear because she always smiled at me, but I've no idea even now whether I did or said the right thing.*

What DO you say to someone who is dying? It is the feeling of being powerless in the face of so much emotional pain that seems to strike a chord in many people. We want to reach out and help and yet feel so impotent when looking for a way to do so. We may wait for the person themselves to bring up the subject. We may constantly search for the 'right moment' or 'the right words'. Perhaps we may feel it is better to avoid the whole subject since it is so awkward. We will fill our visit with inconsequential chatter to 'take their mind off things' or 'cheer them up'.

If you do not know what to say (and why should you?) then how about saying, 'I don't know what to say'?

You could also say simply, 'I am so sorry. Is there anything I can do to help you?'

If you are not sure whether the person who is at the end of life wishes to discuss it you could say, 'Would you like to talk?' You need not say what about. If someone wants to talk and you ask such a direct question, they will surely talk about what is on their mind or, if they don't want to talk, they will say 'No thank you.' If you feel unable to ask in such a direct manner you could try an alternative approach. 'Would you like me to watch the television with you (or read to you) or shall we just talk quietly?'

The least helpful response is to be dismissive. Sometimes this is done with the best of intentions. Perhaps the feeling is that to acknowledge that someone is approaching death will hasten the end. Sometimes dismissing someone's legitimate query is an attempt to deny the truth to ourselves. Sometimes it may be true that when asked 'Am I dying?' we do not know the answer.

If you are a carer, relative or friend and someone at the end of life asks you, 'Am I dying?' try to resist the instinctive reply, 'Of course not. Don't be morbid. Don't be absurd. You'll outlive us all. You are getting better.'

Instead you could say, 'Why do you ask?' which would allow the person to voice any fears they have. The answers may surprise you. Not everyone is afraid of death but most people do not want to die leaving unfinished business.

> *A few days before he died of cancer my husband asked me if the end was near. I managed to resist telling him everything was fine and asked him why he wanted to know. He said, 'Will you make sure my brother knows?'*
>
> *He and his brother had fallen out and hadn't spoken to each other for two years.*

If someone suspects that death is near they may want to make peace with someone, they may want to spend time in a particular place, they may want to know that you will manage after they are gone, they may simply want to know whether they will be kept pain-free. You will not know what their concern is if you simply dismiss their question and try to pretend that there is nothing wrong.

> *My Auntie Nellie said a couple of days before she died, 'Sandra, I'm going to die soon, aren't I?' I asked her why she thought this and she said, 'My Mum and Vi [her dead sister] came to see me last night. They said they'd wait for me outside.' I really did not know what to say. So I just said, 'That's nice.'*

Suppose it is you – the carer, the friend, the relative – you, the 'visitor', who wants to make peace? It may be that you feel guilty or sad about something in the past, perhaps an incident where you behaved badly or acted unjustly, or perhaps about a time when you did not help when it was possible for you to have done so. Perhaps you are a spouse or a partner who feels sad or guilty about the relationship you have experienced with the person at the end of life. Perhaps you are a child who feels you have wronged your dying parent. Close contact with the end of life may cause any of us to feel that we should make peace, or 'tidy up loose ends' or even 'achieve closure'. You may be wondering if there is a 'right way' to do this.

Perhaps the simplest way is by a direct approach. You could say, 'I want to say that I am sorry about such and such. I didn't act the way I should have done.' You will need to be prepared for a possibly unexpected response. Proximity to the end of life may not guarantee a gracious reaction. Perhaps the reply may be, 'You are only saying that because you know I am dying!' How would you react then?

Remember that it is YOU who is choosing to try to 'make peace'. You may get an unexpected response, but you are trying to reach out. So you can try not to allow your attempt at reconciliation to become an opportunity to renew an old quarrel. If you have a response such as that above it is best to just repeat that you are trying to say you are sorry, that you do not want to cause any further upset and then change the subject or perhaps make your escape! You can at least feel justified in trying your best. If on the other hand the response is positive and thankful then you have indeed 'made your peace'.

If you are a spouse or partner with a past difficult relationship to regret, then it is important to realise that you cannot solve all the difficulties of the past with one 'end-of-life apology'. You can, however, say truly that you are sorry your relationship was a bad one, that you know you cannot resolve things in the time left but that you want to concentrate on the parts of the past that were good and pleasant. Even if we feel that we were in no way to blame for the disintegration of a past relationship we can say that we are sorry that it didn't last.

When my ex-husband was dying from a brain tumour and we all knew it was a matter of time I flew over to see him. It was a very unwelcome expense but I knew he had always been in love with me and that I had hurt him very badly by leaving him. When I went to the hospital his eyes lit up when he saw me. I found it very hard to say, 'I'm sorry that things didn't work out between us', because I had never regretted for a moment leaving him, but I felt very sad

> *that I had caused him so much pain. He said, 'It would have been nice if it had worked out,' and I bit back my usual response and just said, 'Yes it would.' We spent the afternoon holding hands and reminiscing. It was very special considering that up to that point there had been a great deal of bitterness between us. Now I am so grateful that I made the effort to go and see him. It was very important for him – but I have to say also for me. Tying up loose ends is also important for the living.*

There is of course justification for the emphasis on pain control at the end of life. Without pain control there cannot be any quality to the end of life, but if the inner spirit is in pain or turmoil there is no amount of physical pain control that will give the patient relief or peace. On the other hand, even to someone not afraid of the 'beyond' the physical details of dying may be most important.

> *My dad had severe heart problems and difficulty breathing. He was a devout Catholic and had seen the priest and received the sacrament and I remember him saying to me, 'Margaret, I'm not afraid of dying. I know God will receive me, but I don't want to die fighting for my every breath!'*

A hospice nurse with 22 years of experience said, 'I never cease to be amazed at how profoundly a person's perceptions and beliefs about what is going to happen to them after they die affect the quality of the last few moments of their life.'

The person who is at the end of life is a whole person. They have a physical, a mental, and a spiritual dimension. Equal attention should be given on this, the final journey, to each of these dimensions. Everyone should be able to die with a pain-free body, a quiet mind and a sustained spirit.

My son bears an uncanny resemblance to my brother, who moved to Australia when he was 20 and cut off all relations with the family. My mother, who suffered from depression from that time, never spoke about my brother nor allowed a word of criticism against him but when she was dying we all sat with her and my son sat at her bedside for her last hours. My mother was convinced this was my brother and just before she died she smiled at him and said quietly, 'I knew you would come back.' We all agreed that this belief gave her the peace of mind that she had lacked for the last 40 years.

Further sources of help and information

The Samaritans
The Samaritan service is available to those in emotional distress
Telephone: 08457 90 90 90
Website: www.samaritans.org

Friends Reunited
Finding old friends/workmates etc
Website: www.friendsreunited.co.uk

Social networking sites
These may enable you to reconnect with people you once knew.
Website: www.facebook.com
Website: www.myspace.com

CHAPTER 3

CARING FOR CARERS — LOOKING AFTER YOURSELF

When you are the carer of someone who is near the end of life it can easily happen that you ignore your own needs and forget your own well-being. The needs of the person you are caring for seem paramount and your own well-being takes a back seat in the urgency of giving all the love and attention that you can to them. Sometimes in the back of your mind you may realise that you are neglecting yourself but you probably tell yourself that this doesn't matter – that for the present time the person near the end of life needs your all and that there will be time to look to your own welfare later. It may even seem selfish to think about your own needs or to consider taking any time to yourself.

You need to remember that you do matter. It will be easier to cope if you look after your own health and well-being. If you are stressed and harassed, if you are feeling tired and unwell, you cannot do your best for the person you are caring for. If you become seriously ill or exhausted, you will not be able to focus your mind properly and you will not be able to cope with the physical demands which may be made on you at this time. Whilst it is true that adrenaline can sometimes carry you through a crisis, it cannot nurture the body or the soul and eventually resources will run out. You will be 'running on empty'.

There are things you can do to look after yourself, but the first and most important of these is to recognise the need to nurture your own welfare. If you are strong in yourself, you can be strong for someone else when you need to be. Looking after your own welfare is not selfish.

It is vital for you and for the one you care for. You may neglect yourself because you think that taking time for your own well-being will make others think less of you. Be assured that those who love you will not do that. Anyone who does not realise that you need to care for yourself throughout this stressful time is not someone whose opinion you need to take notice of.

Looking after yourself involves simple things – things that we interleave into our lives without thinking about them when times are 'normal'. Your mind and body can manage without these things in an emergency; they cannot manage without care in the longer term. You need to give attention to:

- Your physical well-being
- Your emotional well-being
- Accessing the help you need
- How to cope with conflicting demands.

Physical well-being

When we are well and not stressed, we probably don't think about our physical health at all. When caring for someone who is seriously ill or near the end of life, it is easy to ignore physical symptoms that indicate something is wrong with us because our entire concern is for the person we are caring for.

When Peter was really ill, friends and family would often ask me, 'How are you? Are you keeping well?' I would usually answer that I was fine, and I often thought: 'I don't matter. It's Peter who they should be asking about.' Now I realise that they were able to see the strain I was under and they were naturally concerned. They weren't being uncaring about Peter, but they were being caring about me. Unfortunately I wasn't able to see this at the time and I think I was often quite brusque in my replies.

It is, however, vital to remember that you cannot look after the person you are caring for properly if you are unwell yourself. To keep physically well, a person needs to eat well, drink enough (preferably water), get sufficient rest and exercise, and get treatment for small physical problems so that they do not evolve into major illness.

Diet

At this stressful time you should ensure that you are eating well. However, do not add to your stress by worrying overmuch about fashionable (minor) dietary recommendations that keep appearing in the media; it really isn't vital that you count your fruit and vegetable portions daily, drink a set volume of liquid or spend time trying to remember which species count as 'oily fish'. The best way to make sure that you are eating properly is to have a good varied diet. This means not always having the same snatched sandwich because it is the quickest and easiest thing to prepare or forgetting to eat a proper meal yourself because you are busy preparing small attractive portions for the person you are caring for. Try to have three meals each day and vary them, even if varying means something as simple as: 'Chicken on Monday, fish on Tuesday, tuna pasta on Wednesday...'

A large ratatouille-type vegetable mix is very easy to make and freeze in portions and you can easily add this mix to another dish so that it doesn't become tedious. Freezers come into their own in stressful times, and when you cook for the person you are caring for, make extra large portions to freeze for days that you can't find the energy to cook. Soups are another basic, warming, filling food, are easy to freeze and can be hugely comforting to have when you need a quick standby.

Drink whenever you feel thirsty and don't allow other duties to prevent you having a pleasant cup of tea or coffee or a glass of water at intervals, whenever you feel the need. Keep sensible snacks easily available so that you do not have to grab a chocolate bar for an instant energy lift. Some useful snacks and easy-to-prepare meals are listed opposite:

- Cereal bars
- Whole-meal sandwiches with tuna, cheese, ham and tomato or other salad item
- Whole-wheat digestive biscuits
- Eggs in any form (quick to prepare and wholesome)
- Pasta (preferably whole-meal) with ready-prepared (or make up a large batch of tomato-based sauce and freeze portions) sauce and grated cheese
- Thick soup with bread/rolls
- Whole-wheat cereal with milk

You should also make time to sit down and eat your meal quietly and in as relaxed a manner as possible. There are many ways to arrange this. You could ask a friend or other family member to cover you for the period of time whilst you eat. You could occasionally go out to eat during the time you have for yourself (more below). You could time your meals so that they coincide with the times when the person you are caring for is sleeping or when nurses or carers are taking over. Of course, you may wish to share mealtimes with the person you are caring for and they may want you to do this. Provided this does not involve you in extra stress (for example, if you have continually to be alert that the person you are caring for is not choking), then meals can be a pleasant time of sharing and being together. If, however, you have to be continually alert whilst you are assisting someone to eat, then it is a good idea to have at least one of your meals alone and in as stress-free an environment as possible.

Rest

We all need rest from our daily work, and caring for the person you love *is* your daily work. You should try to make sure that you have enough sleep. There are two main causes of sleep disturbance.

Your sleep may be continually disturbed because the person you are caring for needs attention at night. If this is the case, try to arrange things so that giving the required help and attention is as easy as possible. Have adequate lights and make sure that any equipment or changes of clothes/ bed-linen etc are close to hand. Have loose warm clothes for yourself (a tracksuit, for example) which you can pull on quickly, available near your bed, so that you can be warm whilst attending to the person you are caring for, and slip off easily to return to bed. That way you can get up, give the required attention and return to sleep with as little disturbance as possible. If you are in this situation and your sleep is disturbed every night, then you should try to arrange to have at least one night per week when someone else is on 'night duty' so that you can be undisturbed. The alternative is to arrange to sleep away from home once a week or so whilst someone else takes over. Sometimes a friend or another member of the family can undertake this to give you a break, but if this is not possible then it is worth discussing the problem with the doctor or community nurse, who will be able to refer you to a source of help. There are 'night sitting' nursing services and care agencies who provide this help and your doctor or community nurse will know how to access them. You should not 'suffer in silence' as your health and energy level are important for the welfare of the one you are caring for.

The other usual cause of sleep disturbance is worry and stress, which may make you unable to sleep even though your nights are not being disturbed. Anything that affects your life will also affect your sleep. Even when the day is filled with caring and distractions, the night can be a haven for unresolved problems and nagging doubts that you do not have time to think about during the day. If you have trouble sleeping and this lasts for long periods of time, please see your GP, who may be able to refer you to a specialist, help you determine the cause of your insomnia, or even prescribe a medication that can help in the short term. A lack of sleep can initially sound like a small problem, but after a long period of time with little or none, the consequences to other areas of life can be quite significant. It is important to find out why you are not sleeping and address the issues that arise.

Your emotional well-being

Try to find the time to relax. You may feel tired and exhausted and flop into a chair, but that does not mean you are relaxed! In order to relax you need to be able to switch your mind away from the routine worries which you are carrying. A few moments of relaxation will help you make sense of the day and render you better able to cope. Some people find that specific disciplines such as Yoga are really helpful when trying to switch off and relax. Others prefer their relaxation time to be unstructured – perhaps an outing with friends, or a quiet time watching a light and undemanding television programme or listening to music. You should do what seems to work for you, but you should timetable your relaxation time into your life. It is not self-indulgence; it is self-preservation! Always remember that you cannot give of your best to anyone unless you are properly rested yourself. As much as the person who is approaching the end of life needs support, so you, the carer, also need support. Many troubles and worries may be going through your mind – perhaps questions like these:

- What is going to happen?
- How long until he or she dies?
- Will the event be frightening?
- Will I be able to cope?
- What if he/she is in pain? Who will help him/her?
- What shall I do without him/her?
- How will I tell the children/other dependants?

Always remember that there is someone who can help with all these questions and worries. The website for this book (endoflifebook.com) contains a link as to where you are likely to find others who are in a similar position to yourself and with whom you may be able to share your thoughts. One of the biggest challenges that carers face is the loneliness and isolation. The world shrinks into the rooms that the person you are caring for occupies, or the distance between your home and the hospital bed. As time passes, the novelty of visiting wears off and many friends and even family fall by the wayside. It may also be worth checking if it is possible to set up support groups in your area, and if you cannot meet others in the same/similar position face to face, being able to have regular conversations on the phone, in which you may be able to share your feelings and thoughts, may be an important outlet. The Samaritans are also always accessible by either email or telephone, or if there is a branch near you, also face to face. There is a perception that the service is only for people who are suicidal, but this is not correct. The Samaritans are there for anyone in severe emotional distress, and there are times when carers will unquestionably come into this category. They are available 24 hours a day, so if your thoughts and fears seem overwhelming in the early hours of the morning, there is always someone to listen with an empathetic ear.

The help you need

Many people find it difficult to share concerns and ask for help, believing it will be seen as a sign of weakness. Knowing your abilities and your limitations will make you more effective and better able to cope with life's demands. Delegating is a skill, not a weakness. It is also important to remember that your friends and family want to help. How often have you yourself known that someone was in trouble and wondered how you could help them? Perhaps you were wary of asking what you could do to help because you did not want to intrude in a time of trouble. Often friends and family feel helpless, not knowing what to do to help.The best thing you can do is to ask for help in specific areas. Make direct requests – for example, 'I need to get a haircut. Can you find time to sit with X whilst I go for the appointment?' Or perhaps, 'I'm finding it really difficult to get to the shops. Would you mind picking up the items on this list when you are next shopping?' Or you could ask, 'I'd like to get out of the house and get some exercise. Can you come for a walk with me? Or sit with X while I go for a walk?'

People are usually glad to be of service and making a specific request helps them to put aside the time to fit their own schedule. Often friends and neighbours or other family members will make a vague offer – something like, 'Do let me know if there is anything I can do to help'. This is your cue to make a specific request in the way shown above. Do not simply thank them and leave it in the air. If you can't make a specific request at that moment because you are too distracted, say, 'Thank you very much. I do need help with some things. Can I get back to you soon?' This lets those who offer know that you have taken their offer on board and that you will make a request in the near future. In short, remember:

- People want to help
- People respond better to specific requests
- You will be of more use if you are properly supported and rested
- Asking for help is a positive thing to do.

There are also many professionals who can help you and services which you can access to help with specific needs. Your primary sources of help could be your GP and the community nurse. These two professionals should be able to give you information about the many services available – for example, a home nursing service (such as cancer care nurses), free dressings and incontinence aids, or information about your local hospice. Some services are not well advertised and you may never even have heard that they are available, but the community nurse should be able to tell you all about them. In addition to professionals, there are many voluntary services that offer help, aids and equipment, sometimes free, sometimes for a small charge. (Many of the services and sources of help are listed in the reference section for this chapter.)

Guilt

Guilt seems to be generic – something we all have to learn to live with or to hide from. Sometimes no matter what we do for the person we are caring for and no matter how much effort we make, we cannot feel it is enough and need to find a reason to feel guilty. We magnify the importance of each failing. Each imagined failing mounts up and weighs us down. We are probably quite unaware of the effect this can have on our mental health. Guilt can lead to anxiety and depression. Being aware of it sitting on your shoulder, waiting for a moment to be noticed, may be the first step to confronting it.

If you are able to do so, one positive first step is to dissect the content of the guilt. Is it based on a feeling of being out of control? (There is nothing you can do to prevent this life from coming to an end and so you feel guilty.) If so, try instead to concentrate on the things you can control – for example, is there anything you can do to make the person at the end of life feel more comfortable or to take away their anguish? Do you feel able to do this and what steps do you need to take? If not, then can you ask someone else (a close friend or relative, a priest or minister of religion, a Macmillan nurse, a doctor...) to take on this task? If there is no one who can ease the way, perhaps we can let that burden go – it is not something we can control. That way we are not going to fail before we start.

Alternatively, is your feeling of guilt based upon being unable to forgive?

When my ex-husband was terminally ill I went to see him. I wanted to tell him that I forgave him for the way that he had treated me – and I was able to do this, but when it came to forgiving him for the way he had treated our children the words stuck in my throat. Later I realised that it was not up to me to forgive him; it was up to them.

The ability to forgive is a gift. It is not given to everyone. There is a saying, 'to understand is to forgive', but it is not entirely true. It is perhaps easier to say that we should not judge. For us to judge those for whom forgiveness is not an option would mean that first we have to walk a mile or preferably a life time in their shoes. We read in the newspapers from time to time of the parents of a murdered child who forgive the murderer and then we wonder, 'If they can find forgiveness in their hearts, cannot we too?' Or perhaps we feel that they are some kind of saint and that we are not saints. If you feel that there is something that you can never forgive – some action from the past which concerned the person whose end of life is near – then why not just acknowledge that you are unable to forgive that action and move on? It does not necessarily mean that you cannot care for that person and be at their side through their last days. To live with anger or bitterness can be a poison that affects your whole life and touches all relationships – it can destroy them.

Is the guilt based on your past relationship with the person whose life is near its end? If so, it might be appropriate to say to the person, 'I'm sorry that our relationship hasn't always been happy/kind/as we would have liked,' but you would need to be prepared if the reply is not what you had hoped for. Remember that you cannot take responsibility for other people's reactions but you can take responsibility for yours.

The effort of saying 'I'm sorry' is often worthwhile whether we feel responsible for the past or not. Even if you do not feel that you are to blame for problems with a relationship, you may still be sorry that the problems arose. Being left with a lifetime of 'I wish' is a heavy burden and one that we can try to avoid. When someone dies unexpectedly the luxury of having the opportunity to make peace in connection with the past is taken from us.

Allowing the person who is dying to speak of important matters is a gift that we can give. It may be hard to do this. It is very easy to change the subject when a sensitive issue arises. It is very easy to get up from where you are sitting and find something that suddenly seems vitally important to do like straightening the sheets or changing the water in the vase. Usually it is an unconscious action motivated by a deeply uncomfortable feeling when talking about matters that have long been buried. It can be difficult to face certain things from the past, to allow feelings long buried to surface, or to re-address matters that you had hoped were put away for ever. If you are able to, stop, take a deep breath and allow the conversation to take place. You may find that you feel a huge weight has been lifted from your shoulders. Sometimes you don't need to do more than say a quiet word of comfort, or give a squeeze of the hand. It is not always necessary to find the 'right words', and sometimes there are no 'right words' to say. However, avoiding such conversation may lead to many sleepless nights and more guilt.

Expressing your feelings

Sometimes it is hard to voice an emotion even though you may feel deeply. Men particularly may find it difficult to do this. Many men feel that they demonstrate their love, for example, by their actions, by working hard to bring in an income, by doing the DIY jobs, by taking out the rubbish and so on. We need to dispense with the myth that saying 'I love you' has to be a full blown stage production, complete with violins and a setting sun.

One reason that many people hesitate to say these important words is not only that they feel they are unable to say them, but that they feel that there is a kind of drama that has to surround them. When it comes to the end of life, people often fear two things. They may think that if they say 'I love you', they will in some way be signalling the end, or hastening the end of that person's life – tempting fate if you like. Or they may fear that by expressing the emotion they are making their loved one believe that they are close to the end. Such fears may cause any of us to put off revealing simple loving thoughts. Yet if the person does die before we have put these thoughts into words, we may spend the rest of our lives wishing that we had spoken.

Yet another, and just as important, reason for not speaking for some people is that they don't really know how to express their love. It seems so dramatic to sit by someone's bed and say 'I love you'. It is also 'not British' and many families explain that they just 'don't say things like that'. However, the end-of-life journey demands words and actions that are not in our everyday repertoire, and it's no good waiting until the plane doors have closed and the flight is about to take off before you decide it's time to speak out.

One way to express this feeling is to remove the drama from the words. You can say the words in a light manner – for example, 'Bye, Mum. See you tomorrow – love you.' This may be a much easier way of saying that you love your mother, than if you were sitting by her bedside, holding her hand, looking into her eyes, taking a deep breath and saying, 'I love you, Mum.'

> *When my mother was in the hospice. I wanted to say 'I love you' to her but I felt that if I did I would in some way hasten the end of her life. I put it off and put it off and one day a member of the staff said to me, 'If you want to tell her that you love her – now would be a good time.' I still couldn't say it, believing that once I had she would die. The staff member then said to me, 'You don't have to make a big deal of it. As you leave just say "Bye, Mum. See you tomorrow. Love you, Mum".'*
>
> *So I did it exactly the way that she had told me. It felt very natural, and thank God, because my mother died that night, and if I had waited another day it would have been too late. I would have had to live with it for the rest of my life.*

Saying it in such a casual way also helps if the person at the end of life is in denial. Some people prepare themselves for the end, but others remain in a state of denial and don't wish to discuss end-of-life arrangements or to express any suggestion that they might not be around in the future. This is their way of dealing with such an event, and it is a valid way for them. We are all so different in our approach. Some people will plan a trip months and months in advance, checking the best fares, best flights and the hotels that will be best value for money and looking into day trips in great detail and have every moment of the holiday planned months in advance. Others get to within a couple of weeks of their annual leave and start to think about where they want to go. Each one of us approaches and reacts to events in life and the end of life differently and each one of us brings to it our psychological make-up, our personality, background, history, attitudes and fears.

If you really cannot bring yourself to say the vital three words, perhaps you can write them. A short letter left by the bed, a card with the words 'We all love you so much', or a posy of flowers with a card saying 'All our love', may help you express this sentiment in a way you feel is appropriate. Or perhaps you might send in something you have made or bought – a knitted bed jacket with a card saying: 'With all my love'; a book inscribed: 'I bought this because I know you love xxx and I love you'; or perhaps, if you prefer, a recorded message for the person at the end of life to listen to when you have left.

So much of this chapter has been devoted to 'love' because it is really important that the person who is at the end of life knows that he or she is loved. It is important for all of us. Money can buy you many things, but it 'can't buy you love'. Love is the one thing that we all long for, that we all want our families and friends to feel towards us, and it is the one thing that may make the ups and downs of our lives feel worthwhile. If we are not loved, if we cannot measure our relationships in some degree by that sentiment, we can be left with a sense of emptiness as we make our exit.

So if you do love the person who is at the end of life – please tell them this, in whatever way you are able, not only for their sake but also for yours.

Love seeketh not itself to please
Nor for itself hath any care
But for another gives its ease
And builds a heaven in hell's despair.

William Blake

Spending time with the person who has died

> One of the staff at the hospice said to my father, brother, sisters and myself, 'Perhaps you would each like to spend some time alone with your mother.' She said this to us after my mother had died.
>
> I am still so grateful to her. I would have felt embarrassed to ask the rest of my family if they minded my spending some time alone with my mother. It would have looked as though I was different or felt special in some way. When the nurse said it, it was as though she gave each of us permission and we didn't have to feel awkward.
>
> My brother didn't want to do this, but my father and my sisters and I each went in alone and it was so helpful. However, two days later when I went to the undertakers and saw my mother lying there, it was a shock; it was as though she was no longer my mother but a cold stranger. I was sorry that I had seen her again. It was as though whatever had made her the person that she was had gone, and what was left was a shell. When my grandmother died two years later I again sat with her immediately after she had died, but did not want to see her again after that. I really believe that immediately after death the soul, or whatever makes the person who he or she was, is still present or at least hasn't completely left the body.

If death takes place in a hospital, then the nursing staff will usually be glad to make arrangements for you to spend time with the person who has died. Unfortunately, it may not be possible to arrange for this time to be in a private room and the best you may be able to expect is a curtained bed for limited privacy. After death in a nursing or a care home, the staff will usually be able to arrange for you to spend time with the person who has died in their own room. If death takes place at home the funeral directors will move the body only when you agree that the time is right. You do not have to call or notify funeral directors until you are ready to do so.

I wasn't with my father when he died, although my brother and sisters were. When I visited a few days later I decided to go and see him at the undertakers. When we walked in to the chapel of rest I thought they had laid out the wrong person! It didn't look like my father at all. When later my mother, my mother-in-law and my father-in-law died I chose not to see them after death. The previous experience was so unpleasant that I felt it better to remember them as they had been when alive.

When my husband died I saw him almost immediately afterwards. I remember it was traumatic but also comforting. He was still warm and I was able to hold his hand and I felt that I had time to say goodbye. Even though I knew he was dead it was as if his 'essence' was still around. I am glad I chose to see him.

If you wish to spend time alone, or in the company of close family members and friends, with the person who has died, then do so. Take all the time you need and do not let yourself be hurried for others' convenience or for convention's sake. If, on the other hand, spending time with the person who has died is upsetting and traumatic and you do not wish to do this, then do not feel pressured to do what others urge. The chapter on funeral arrangements gives further guidance on what happens after death.

One of my closest friends is a reformed alcoholic and lives near San Francisco. I wrote her a very lengthy email and told her of my mother's illness, all the stresses and strains between the family and our conflicting views on her care and received an email back almost immediately. She wrote just five words: 'One day at a time.'

I know this is the philosophy of AA but I was extremely irritated that I had unburdened myself to her at great length and only received these five words back so I wrote to her again, explaining in greater detail how difficult it was to be torn in so many different directions by all the family disagreements, my guilt at not being able to do more, visit more often, and ease her pain. Again I got an email in return, this time with six words: 'Take one day at a time.'

I decided I was no longer going to share my anguish with her, if this was all she could manage, and I threw myself into caring for my mother and battling through all the emotional demons that seemed to crawl out of the woodwork. Every now and then my friend would send an email saying: 'Remember, just take one day at a time.'

I don't know how long it took me to realise the wisdom of those words and if I had listened earlier they would probably have saved me from an enormous amount of unnecessary stress. Every day I did the best I could for my mother. I took each day at a time, and the truth was nearly all my long-term fears about my mother were groundless because she died much more suddenly and peacefully than we had anticipated.

Professional carers need to take care of themselves in the same way as private carers. The nature of their work and the length of their working hours make taking care of themselves a priority if they are to remain effective in the workplace.

Care workers should remember that they too need to pay attention to a nutritious diet, to adequate rest and relaxation and to caring for their own health. Putting diesel in a petrol tank will cause the motor to stop functioning. Non-nutritious food and lack of rest and of suitable exercise will have the same effect on a human body and this usually shows itself in the form of days off work with ill health, depression and a general feeling of lethargy.

The seemingly endless amount of paperwork that dogs the footsteps of professional carers, as well as their interactions with clients and clients' families, means that they are often put under a lot of strain. It is true that family carers cannot go home at the end of the day to unwind. However, the work of professional carers continues, sometimes for years, so the knock-on effect of their not taking proper care of themselves can be long term.

Carers usually have to attend many training events as part of their induction before they commence working, and several more during each working year, but these seldom include training in how to take care of themselves. The clients' or residents' needs are continually assessed but the care workers' are not.

> *I work for Age UK (formerly Age Concern) and I am also a family carer as I am taking care of my mother who has Alzheimer's and my father who has Parkinson's. I found ELM's* workshop amazing. It was actually very informative and really gave us all an insight into people who have behaviour viewed as challenging; really very good, thank you. I also found the end of the session really helpful – especially the part about the importance of laughter and tears and the emphasis you place on taking care of ourselves. It is a really important subject. I don't think anyone else ever mentions it.*
>
> * see page 65.

Recognition of the physical and emotional needs of care workers is key to a healthy workforce and a healthy workforce is key to continuity of care. Continuity of care is one of the keys to satisfied clients (or 'service users', as they are called in the care industry), which is the desired outcome for all care providers. So perhaps it is time their needs were taken into consideration?

Further sources of help and information

Crossroads
Aims to give carers a break from their caring responsibilities
Tel: 0845 450 0350 (or local offices)
Website: www.crossroads.org.uk

The Samaritans
The Samaritans service is always available on the telephone to those in emotional distress
Tel: 08457 90 90 90
Website: www.samaritans.org

Carers UK
Provides information and advice to carers
Tel: 0808 808 7777
Website: www.carersuk.org

Princess Royal Trust for Carers
Information and advice for carers
Tel: 0844 800 431
Website: www.carers.org

ELManagement Ltd
Training in all aspects of social care
Website: www.ELManagement.org

Many specific societies give support to carers as well as people with the relevant medical condition. The following is a selected list:

Macmillan Cancer Support
Tel: 020 7840 7840
Website: www.macmillan.org.uk

Marie Curie Cancer Care
Tel: various local numbers
Website: www.mariecurie.org.uk

PALLS
Palliative care at home.
Tel: 01420 475 057
Website: www.palls.co.uk

St David's Foundation
Hospice care
Tel: 01633 271364
Website: www.stdavidsfoundation.co.uk

Parkinsons Disease Society
Tel: 0808 800 0303
Website: www.parkinsons.org.uk

Alzheimer's Society
Tel: 0207 423 3500
Website: www.alzheimers.org.uk

Multiple Sclerosis Society
Tel: 0808 800 8000
Website: www.mssociety.org.uk

Motor Neurone Disease Association
Website: www.mndassociation.org

CHAPTER 4

END OF LIFE IN HOMES AND HOSPITALS

Most of us think that we would like to die at home 'quietly in my sleep'. However, the fact is that many people end their lives in a care home, or a nursing home, a hospital or a hospice.

Residential and nursing homes for the elderly are a microcosm of the wider world and their attitude to the end of life very much reflects that of the outside world. All of us would like to be treated with dignity and respect in our last days. Equally, we would like to see those we love treated with dignity and respect as they approach the end of life. We all agree that this is the basic minimum that we can offer all older people. We note those words when we read about government initiatives for older and vulnerable people. We see those words when we look at the mission statements for homes of all types, and to their credit many do treat their residents at the end of life with dignity and respect. Many homes offer all possible facilities to friends and relatives of the dying so that death can be a peaceful and dignified experience.

And many homes do not.

Most care workers mean well. They enjoy the extraordinary job they do (and they certainly don't do it for the pay or the status) and they try to look after residents to the best of their ability. However, care workers are likely to feel just as much awkwardness when talking about the end of life as the rest of the population. Although all care workers and managerial staff in care and nursing homes should receive training in end-of-life care and bereavement, the sad truth is that many do not.

Mostly they are given leaflets to read, distance learning or e-learning. This type of training is convenient for ticking the boxes but woefully inadequate in caring for the emotional needs of staff or assisting them in caring for the needs of the residents and their families. According to the National Audit Office Data collected by Skills for Care in 2007, as few as seven per cent of care-home workers and five per cent of nursing-home workers have an NVQ level 3 qualification which includes *optional* training in supporting people at the end of life. Staff turnover rates also suggest that care homes are training fewer staff than they lose on an annual basis.

However, even the best training cannot make up for staffing problems, for difficult staff relationships, for a staff member having the proverbial 'bad day' or for unusual and unforeseen circumstances arising. Attracting staff is difficult enough due to the low wages and the generally undeserved bad publicity that carers receive. To complicate matters further, in many parts of the UK, CRB checks (Criminal Record Bureau) can take between four and 16 weeks to clear (and in some cases where there are multiple police forces concerned it can take longer) and staff must be constantly supervised until these checks have been completed. This can leave crucial vacancies unfilled and may put off new staff from joining. Most people do not want to wait months before starting a new position. When it is our close friend or relative who receives slapdash care, is left in pain or is treated in an undignified manner, we don't usually consider these factors. Even if we do make allowances, this does not make up for the dissatisfaction we may feel and the guilt and upset which we may carry with us long afterwards.

Staff in any care home should gather as much information about a new resident as possible when they initially arrive, or immediately before admission. Along with very important life history questions, care staff should also ask questions about personal preferences in every area of life from favourite colours to preferred bathing time. Included among these questions, the important end-of-life questions could be slottted to diffuse some of the anxiety and distress out of both asking the questions and answering them.

Sometimes it is a close family member who needs to be asked these questions. Some people with advanced dementia or with severe learning difficulties may not understand such questions or may not be able to give considered answers. But the questions should always be asked. If staff do not ask you such things or do not take a proper life and family history when you or the person you are caring for enters the home, then you may like to reconsider your choice of home!

The fact is that many care workers find it very difficult to ask residents questions about plans for their end of life. No one feels comfortable asking whether the resident has thought about these issues – whether they want to be buried or cremated, and if they have made their end-of-life wishes known. The general attitude is that: 'You can't ask someone that question when they have just entered the home.' The alternative of asking when someone has been in the home for some time can be even more distressing for residents, who may believe that they have not been given important information about their health. Equally, many care workers find the same difficulty in explaining to friends and family that the person they love is near the end of life.

Questions about the end of life should be asked and the answers should be recorded. If you are helping someone to settle into a residential or nursing home, then you can make sure that the staff have information about these essential end-of-life questions. These details should be recorded on notes and in care plans.

It is very important to maintain close and cordial relationships with the staff of the home. Whether voluntarily or through necessity, you have decided to hand over the daily care of the person you have been looking after to others. This can make you feel very defensive and guilty and may make you over critical or very ready to find fault with the care given. Try to remember that (as stated above) the majority of care workers mean well and enjoy caring for others. Most want to do a good job and to make those they care for feel happy and secure. It is worth getting to know those with whom you will come into contact most and building a good relationship. We are all human and it is human to try just that little bit harder for someone whom we find pleasant and approachable. Care workers have a very challenging job, not only physically; they are also overburdened with paperwork, legally required to record all aspects of the care they provide. They usually work long hours and, as we mentioned before, their salaries are often lower than those of people stacking shelves in some supermarkets. Their job satisfaction and your appreciation are very important to them and help to compensate for the low wages.

This does not mean that you should never complain about careless treatment or lack of attention. Unless problems are pointed out to staff in a timely manner they have no way of knowing that there *is* a problem. Some things are obviously wrong. Residents in care and nursing homes should not be left in distress due to lack of pain relief. They should be helped to keep clean. They should have good and nourishing food at regular intervals. However, although it may be difficult to accept, the fact is that everyone has different standards when it comes to things like personal hygiene, tidiness, good or bad manners, appropriate clothing and manner of address, and so on. If care workers think it acceptable to put the television on when they settle your uncle in a chair after getting him up in the morning, how will they know he dislikes it unless you (or your uncle) tell them so? If your mother likes to have her mobile phone to hand to telephone you, staff should not leave it on the other side of the room so that she is at risk of falling when trying to reach it. But someone needs to explain that your mother would like the phone left nearby. Care staff are not mind readers and should not be accused of wrong doing or neglect where they have not been informed of residents' likes or dislikes.

If you see evidence that the person you are caring for is being abused or mistreated you should take the matter up immediately and urgently. If you believe that they are being neglected or their treatment does not match up to the standards you and they would like, you should raise the matter at the earliest opportunity. Sometimes it is best to raise matters at the time. For example, suppose you noticed that the person you are caring for was still in night clothes when you visited during the afternoon, although they were well enough to be getting up each day. Naturally you would want to know why. Perhaps the person you are caring for is confused and unable to explain this to you. In this case, the best thing would be to ask one of the care workers in a firm but pleasant manner what the reason was. If you are unhappy with the answer, then you can take the matter further, but it may be that there is a simple explanation.

Consider these approaches:

Approach 1

Question:'I see my husband is still in his pyjamas. I think I have left enough clean clothes. Is there a problem getting him dressed?'

Answer: 'We were expecting the doctor to call to examine him this morning so, although we helped him wash we thought it best to keep him in his pyjamas. Unfortunately the doctor was held up. We are expecting him any minute.'

Approach 2

Question: 'Why on earth isn't my husband dressed? It's very undignified for him wandering around in nightclothes! Surely you've had time to get him up by now?'

Answer: 'Well, I'm sorry about that. We did expect the doctor a bit earlier.'

Question: 'Doctor? What has he got to do with it? Surely it isn't too much to expect you to get people up by the afternoon! I want to talk to the manager!'

The first approach elicits the relevant information without immediately putting the care workers on the defensive.

You should also bear in mind that the Mental Capacity Act means that if the staff believe that the resident has capacity to decide what he or she wants at the time when they are given a choice, the care staff have to respect the resident's decision. So, for example, it may be that the person you are worried about has chosen to stay in his or her night-clothes. Even if you think they should have been made to dress, the staff at the home are only following the terms of the Act in this matter. Just because someone has (for example) a form of dementia, it does not mean that they cannot make their own personal choices and care staff (and you) have to respect this.

If you have discussed a problem with a member of staff and do not feel satisfied, it is perfectly in order to ask to speak to the manager. It is often, however, a good idea to give some notice rather than storming off to the manager's office on the spot. This gives the manager time to talk to staff members and find out just what is behind the problem. It is always difficult to be calm and keep your temper when you believe that the person you care for is not getting the right attention. You will already be under stress and perhaps feeling guilty that you can no longer care for them yourself. However, it really does not help to shout, to use offensive language or to accuse someone of neglect at this point. Ask firmly and politely for a meeting with the manager as soon as possible and explain what your complaint is about. Often the lack of knowledge about the memory loss associated with dementia causes families and friends, quite reasonably, to become extremely distressed when their relative states that no one has brought them breakfast or lunch or assisted them to go to the bathroom.

Dementia training and understanding are not only crucial for care workers and managers but also for family members, and those homes that have identified this need believe that when families are given the basic understanding of the nature of dementia the number of complaints drops. (Dementia is the umbrella term for a number of diseases that affect the structure of the brain. Alzheimer's disease is the most common cause of dementia.)

It is an excellent idea to keep a notebook or diary with you when you visit and to note anything that worries or upsets you at the time. This will allow you to give instances of the things that have been wrong and may allow the manager to work out whether the problem is occurring with a particular member of staff or at a particular time of the day.

If the person you care for is at the end of life, the manager of the home ought to ensure that those closest to them understand this. You and the person you are caring for may already know that death is near, but an acknowledgement from staff and a discussion of the needs of the person whose life is near its end, and of their close family and friends, is important. We have already noted that homes should keep a record of end-of-life wishes. As the time draws nearer, the subject should be addressed again so that everyone (including all care staff – even casual or 'agency' staff) is clear about what may be required. It goes without saying that the home should allow close family unlimited access at this time. Family and friends, in their turn, should respect the need for care staff to ask for space or privacy at certain times when dealing with the physical needs of the person at the end of life. If you, the person closest, feel able to help with intimate physical processes, then by all means tell staff and ask if you can assist. If you don't feel able to do this, do not feel guilty. Use the waiting time to care for yourself (perhaps eating and drinking) and to calm yourself so that you can face the person who is dying without causing them extra distress.

It may help you to remember that the care staff may also be sad at this time. When you care for someone, you do grow fond of them, and helping someone at the end of life, whilst a great privilege, can be very stressful and very sad.

Some homes have an end-of-life 'champion' who takes the lead when a resident dies. She may be, but need not necessarily be, the person who notifies the family. Calling that person the 'champion' seems rather strange. We prefer the name 'end-of-life lead'.

When someone dies, it has an effect on everyone within the home. Unfortunately the 'empty chair syndrome' seems to rule in many places. Edna, who often sits with Joan, sees Joan's chair empty at breakfast but thinks perhaps she is sleeping late. At lunchtime, when her chair is still empty, she asks a care worker, 'Where is Joan? Is she not feeling well?'

only to be told that Joan died during the night. How does Edna feel? Is she not significant enough to be told earlier that her friend has died? Does no one recognise that she will have feelings of sadness and grief? What will happen when Edna dies? Will no one speak of her passing?

There are some homes where a close friend or companion will be told of her friend's passing, but it seems to be fairly hit and miss. There has to be a change in policy so that there is a system in place that automatically triggers certain actions when a resident dies.

The other reason why residents are often not told of their friends' passing is that there is an outdated belief that it will make the resident think about his or her own end of life. Most of the elderly residents not only think about the end of their lives but are in many ways prepared for death. Generally speaking, the older people become the more prepared for death they are. Perhaps their relatives are not ready for them to die, but often they themselves are mentally and emotionally packed and ready for their journey and probably have been for some time.

But the end-of-life lead, or her deputy, should be the one to inform the care workers who had daily contact with (and who probably became attached to) the deceased of a death so that they are told individually in a way that recognises and respects the fact that they are going to be upset or affected. The information should be passed to them in a significant and organised manner, not 'by the way' in passing.

Almost everyone has a mobile phone, so it is not an impossible task to ask the care workers concerned to come to the manager's office or meet with the end-of-life lead when they arrive. They can then be informed with sensitivity of the death. If they are off duty that day, they should be phoned and asked if they need any support. The emotional cost to the care workers cannot be over-estimated if you consider the number of deaths that they will experience. Likewise, the financial impact on the home cannot be over-estimated if you consider the cost of replacing staff who suffer emotional burnout.

Having informed the care workers that the resident has died, the next group of people who need to be told are the residents. Those who suffer from dementia may not remember if they are told, and informing them should be a decision made by the people who know them best (but this does not mean that they should not be told). Any of the residents who have been close to the deceased should be told individually and supported. But it doesn't end there. It may be the end of the life, but it can be the beginning of a process of remembering the deceased and moving on.

There is a very important point here. A resident who sees a deceased companion quickly forgotten will know that when their turn comes they too will be hastily taken out of the back door and their memory erased. We know that the way others are treated will be the way we will be treated too. Where does dignity and respect come in to that?

It is so easy for older people to lose their sense of self-worth. One of the key principles of good mental health is a sense of having a place in the world, a feeling that we have a part to play, a feeling that we contribute to society. It is hard enough for older people to cope with the loss of a friend without demonstrating to them the lack of respect that may happen when they die. They may think that when they die they will be quickly forgotten and life in the home will move on as though they never existed. How can they have any feeling that they matter? How can we make people feel that they are important and give them a sense of self-worth when they know that their life is so unimportant that we will not even make mention of the fact that they have died?

In the best of situations, the residents, the care workers and the families can have the opportunity to grieve together. There are many ways to arrange this. For example, a table can be set up in the lounge with a photo of the person who died. It can be either a recent photo or one taken some time previously with a short life history attached to it. A small book for people to write their memories in can be placed on the table. Information about the funeral can be pinned to a notice board above the table and information about the funeral tea, which can be held at the home after the funeral. A small fresh bouquet of flowers will add an important and inexpensive touch.

A one-minute silence in the dining room can take place either on the day of the death or on the day of the funeral. The residents will know that when their time comes there will be a one-minute silence for them too and they will be remembered.

Crucially, it can be emphasised by the end-of-life lead that conversations about the person who has died are encouraged. It is important to keep the deceased person's name alive. There seems to be a strange belief that if you do not mention the person's name, no one will remember and grieve, but of course all that happens is that no one talks about their sorrow because they think they cause others to be upset when naturally the deceased person may be in everyone's thoughts. It is possible to respect and celebrate someone's life simply by talking about them and remembering them.

Another idea is to set one afternoon in the year aside as a day for remembering everyone who has died. A tea can be held in the home, and the families of those who have died during the year can be asked if they would like to bring either sandwiches, biscuits or a cake. The care workers can attend and meet up again with the families and everyone can remember their family member who passed away during the year. It will be an opportunity for the care workers to meet up again with family members who they possibly became quite close to, for the family members to talk to the care workers about their relative (who perhaps knew them better than anyone else at the end of life), and for the other residents to realise that they too will be remembered. Similarly, it would be nice to plant a tree, or a bush, in memory of all those who died. Again, this is not a big expense in financial terms but the rewards would be felt throughout the home. Dignity and respect will have found a place to reside and that ethos can only benefit all involved.

> *I had the idea of a memorial tree because I wanted the families to know even when their loved ones are gone they are not forgotten. A resident taught me how to make a ribboned cross using a lollipop stick that allows me to burn the resident's name on one side and the date and year they were born and died on the other. I then varnish the sticks four or five times. I try and find out what their favourite colour was so I can colour-coordinate their cross.*

*Last December our first remembrance service took place conduct-
ed by the local reverend. There were 16 crosses on the tree, and
bereaved families were invited. It was an unforgettable day. We
received a plaque from the local funeral directors 'in memory of
those we cared for.'*

*I think the tree encourages the families to come back and visit.
We are going to take photos of the tree and send them out as
postcards to invite the families of those bereaved to come to the
home for a remembrance service.*

Jean Chick, Anglesea Heights Bupa

It may well be that residents will want to say goodbye to a companion who has passed away. It may be that they will want to sit with them
or just say goodbye. Others will not want to. This is such an individual
matter that it can only be covered with a general statement such as:
'Anyone who would like to spend some time with Mavis to say goodbye is welcome to do so.'

It was not even 100 years ago when 90 per cent of people died in
their own homes and were laid out in the parlour. The neighbours would
come to pay their respects and the fact that there was a body lying in the
parlour would not faze the children of the family nor would they find it
strange. They would have grown up with the fact that death is a natural
end of life. All this has changed. We have moved away from the end of
life, and it has become the realm of medicine.

Gone are the days where we carefully and lovingly washed the deceased person and dressed them in their best clothes. Now we give this
task over to strangers. The only connection that younger people have
with death these days is the violent and unnatural death that they read
about or watch on TV.

Care workers' emotions need to be recognised, be they formal
care workers or family carers. This is another important reason why

different types of memorials are essential. It allows everyone to voice their feelings. Some people will always have a bigger impact on those that cared for them than others and often the end of life of one person will have a bigger impact on one care worker than on others. This could be because she or he reminded the care worker of someone that they knew or loved or even a member of their own family. Sometimes, if this is explored, hidden grief may surface and will need to be handled sensitively.

I was on the night shift for five years and used to spend a lot of time talking to Jane. When she first moved in she hated being in the home and lay in bed crying quietly. My gran had died the year before and I was very close to her so I suppose Jane became a sort of substitute. She used to tell me a lot of stuff about the family, about her husband and her daughter who she never really got on with, about her life and was a great listener. I told her stuff that I never told anyone else; I even told her when I had an abortion and couldn't tell my mum or dad. I think I stayed in that job mostly because of her. One night I came on shift and saw that her bed was made and the room looked too tidy so I asked one of the other carers where Jane was. She looked really surprised and a bit embarrassed and said, 'Oh, didn't anyone tell you? She was rushed to hospital at lunchtime and died soon after arrival.' I was devastated and sat on her bed and cried most of the night. I felt that I had lost my gran all over again. But most of all I was really hurt that no one had bothered to tell me that she had died. I left the job soon after that. I felt that nobody cared about my feelings at all. They tell you to care, but when you do, they don't care about you or your feelings.

Many of us reading this book will find ourselves residing in a home towards the end of our lives. We all need to consider how we want the end of our own lives to be approached. It is a good idea to decide now the manner in which we would like the home to remember us after we pass on – lest we be forgot.

Many people, even those who have been able to live out their last few months at home surrounded by family, finally meet death in a hospital. This is really very sad. Hospitals are supposed to be places where we go to 'be cured', to 'get better', and this is how the care is planned. The surprising fact is that nurses and doctors (unless specifically trained in palliative care) do not have very much training in how to look after someone who is dying. According to the National Audit Office, '… only 29 per cent of doctors and 18 per cent of nurses had received any pre-registration training in end-of-life care. In addition, only 39 per cent of doctors and 15 per cent of nurses had received pre-registration training in communicating with patients approaching the end of their life.'

Often the physical care in a hospital is very good. The doctors and nurses understand about pain control. They have been trained in physical care. They know when a patient needs to be washed, encouraged to eat or drink, helped to sit up or to lie down. However, most medical care staff are not trained in the mental, emotional and spiritual care of those near the end of life. Only 54 per cent of general nurses and a third of doctors reported being trained in the use of at least one of the three National Institute for Health and Clinical Excellence (NICE) recommended approaches to end-of-life care (Gold Standards Framework, Liverpool Care Pathway or Preferred Priorities for Care) (National Audit Office, 2008).

Perhaps we should realise here that often the medical staff feel particularly helpless when dealing with the dying. Their job is to make people better, not to ease their passing. They also have a large number of patients to care for and part of their remit is to ensure that nearby patients are not upset by the fact that someone in the next bed or across the ward is dying. Tomorrow they will have to deal with the depression and low morale of those in the ward who are left alive. As with the staff in a care or nursing home, the medical care staff will have to deal with their own grief at the same time as looking after their patients.

If you are close to someone who is near to the end of life in a hospital, it is useful to be aware of these facts. Your concern is for the one you care for and you will want to do the very best you can to make sure that they have all the care, all the attention that they need, that notice is taken of any end-of-life wishes that they have stated, and that family and close friends have the chance to spend some time, perhaps in saying their last goodbye in privacy.

In the best circumstances, everyone near the end of their life will be put in a private room, with unlimited family access and with careful and considerate nursing. But hospitals very seldom are able to provide 'the best circumstances'. Often the last moments are marred by desperate attempts on the part of medical staff to resuscitate. When a crisis happens, the visiting family will almost always be sent away from the bed whilst medical staff work. They may never see their loved one alive again. Death seldom comes quietly and peacefully and even when it does the last moments may be upset by flimsy screens hiding a listening public ward, by clumsy nursing or by an atmosphere so tense that no one afterwards cares to remember the event.

The ambulance was empty and the doors to casualty open. I walked in to a hallway devoid of life, an alarm screaming, a flashing light above a closed door. Although there was no one to ask, I knew my partner was behind that door and the alarm was for us. I never thought to open the door; I suppose I knew it was all over. So I just sat in the empty waiting room and waited. After I don't know how long, someone came and I just pointed to that door. Then a nurse appeared and gave me the classic line, 'We've done all we can.'

Only an hour before, my partner had been short of breath so I had called an ambulance. Earlier he'd had a home visit from a doctor, who gave him a pain killer and said he had back ache. I didn't really believe that because I'd never seen him in such pain. So I thought I'd get him signed up with my GP the next morning. And now it was the next morning, 4 o'clock, and all too late.

However, there are things that can be done to help the situation. If the person you are caring for is taken into hospital for what may be their last days, it is worth, as it is in a care home, getting to know the staff, and keeping on cordial terms with them. Again, this does not mean that you should not complain about neglect or bad treatment. What it does mean is that you should try your best to keep calm, to bring up problems in a reasoned manner and if necessary to take up those problems with the right person. The hospital liaison service, PALS (Patient Advice and Liaison Service), is very useful here. If you enquire they will tell you who you should approach about any particular concern. Sometimes they will make enquiries or intervene on your behalf.

It is particularly important when necessary for you to be the mouthpiece of the person you are caring for. Someone who is very ill can often not raise the energy even to signal that they need a drink, for example. Busy nursing staff are often too distracted. You can draw the attention of staff to the needs of the person who is ill and even offer to care for them yourself where you know you are able to. For example, nursing staff often do not have time to help or encourage people to eat. Most hospitals exclude visitors at meal times, but if the person you are caring for needs to be encouraged or assisted to eat then ask if you can come in at those times specifically for this purpose. Most nursing staff will welcome your assistance in this matter.

If you feel the need for privacy, ask if you can have screens around the bed. In most hospitals, single rooms are few and usually retained for patients with an infection, for example, but there is no harm in asking if the person you are caring for can be moved into one if it is available. You should also not feel awkward in asking to speak to a minister of religion if this is what you want. Most hospitals have a chaplain who works in the hospital and all hospitals should be able to contact a minister of any major religion. If the person at the end of life is no longer able to make their own requests but you know that they would like, for example a priest to administer last rites, then ask for this on their behalf. Make sure that staff are aware of any special religious requirements just as you would make sure they know about any Advance Directive which has been made (see Chapter 1, Practical issues).

When my brother died of lung cancer a few years ago we didn't always find that he received the best standard of care. We found it difficult to get answers to our questions from the various medical staff. For example, he developed a huge thirst shortly before he died and despite asking 'Why?' we never found out the answer. We really felt that the general nursing staff expected us to do much of their work for them and were not particularly empathetic to the fact that we were actually losing a dear brother.

His lung cancer nurse was absolutely wonderful and supported him and us all the way through his short illness. She tended to his needs and, to a certain extent ours, on the day he died. I wish I could say that his death was dignified, but it was far from that. He died in the ward with just a curtain around for privacy as according to the hospital there were no side wards available. (A very high profile person died at the same hospital a few weeks after and my sister cynically questioned whether a side ward became available for him.)

When my father was dying the most ghastly thing was that he was in such a busy hospital ward. The staff said that there was nowhere else to move him and we had to say our last farewells conscious of 'listening ears' outside the screen. It made a difficult time even more stressful and to be honest it still ruins my memories of his last days.

People near the end of life often claim that they can see or have been visited by a dead family member or a friend. This phenomenon is so common that the staff in care homes and hospitals sometimes use it as a sign of imminent death and inform the family that the time is near. There is no need to try to suggest to the person near end of life that they are hallucinating. The images are seldom frightening; indeed, they are often reassuring and comforting. The person you are caring for might say that, 'Mum has come to fetch me,' for example. There is no way for any of us to know whether the person dying is actually seeing the people they describe and it would be presumptuous to argue with them or to suggest they are 'imagining things'. If it upsets you to discuss such a thing you can quietly change the subject. Otherwise it is best just to acknowledge the 'vision' and be glad that it gives comfort.

> *On the day she died my mother kept asking, 'Why is David there?' pointing to the end of the bed. David was my father's name and he had died three years previously. We couldn't see anything, but she didn't seem frightened at seeing him. A few minutes before she died she opened her eyes and half raised her hand as if she was waving at the end of the bed. We are convinced that Dad 'came back' to fetch her.*

> *In the few weeks before she died my mother-in-law kept telling us that her sister had been to see her. We knew she didn't have any sister living but thinking she was a bit confused we just humoured her. Now I wonder!*

There are other clinical signs that the end of life is near and in the best situations hospital staff will explain this to you and reassure you. If you are worried about anything like this you should ask, and persist in asking if you are put off. Remember that (as previously stated) hospital staff are often quite embarrassed that someone is dying rather than 'being cured'. Sometimes you may need to reassure them that you can accept the situation.

After someone has died, hospital staff should allow you as much time as you need to be with them. If attempts have been made to resuscitate or death has taken place whilst hospital procedures have been carried out, then staff may wish to 'tidy' the body before you see it. They are acting in your interests even though you may not be able to accept this at the time. However, you should always ask to be given time alone with the deceased if you wish it. Don't let anyone hurry you or other family members at this time.

> *My mother died before we reached the hospital even though they had called us to say we should come. The thing I remember most was that when we went into the room the nurse had opened the window. It gave me comfort because I remember my old Irish nanny telling me that when someone died you should open the window 'to let the spirit out'. I don't know if this was why the nurse did it, but I remember that it made me feel better at the time.*

Ending life in a hospice is not covered in detail here. The only remit of a hospice is to care for the dying. Their entire focus is on holistic care, understanding that each person's care needs are different. Caring only for that person's physical needs will not be considered sufficient to allow them to have a peaceful passing.

A majority of hospice patients are suffering from cancer. There are two main reasons for this. The first is that much funding comes from the cancer charities and the second is that cancer has a predictable pathway and it is not difficult to give a reasonably accurate prognosis and therefore estimate of the period of stay in the hospice.

There are only 220 hospice and palliative care inpatient units and 3,203 hospice and palliative care beds in the UK, which is why the hospice movement has had to spread out to homes, hospitals and private homes. There are two main hospice movements. One is the NHS Gold Standard Framework (GSF) and the other is the Liverpool Care Pathway (LCP), which is a joint effort between Marie Curie and the Liverpool University Trust. The NHS Gold Standard Framework is more of a systematic approach to optimising the care for patients in the final year of life. The Liverpool Care Pathway is aimed at those whose end of life is more imminent, and where it is agreed by a multidisciplinary team that the person is dying. The aim of these two hospice movements is to improve the quality of care at the end of life for *all patients* and enable more patients to live and die in the place of their choice. Both of these movements are very beneficial and helpful to those in need of palliative care and it is worth finding out whether the home where the person you are caring for resides has a link to either of them.

Further sources of help and information

Liverpool Care Pathway
Website: www.mcpcil.org.uk/liverpool-care-pathway/

Gold Standard Framework
Website: www.goldstandardsframework.nhs.uk

Information on Advance Directives
Website: www.endoflifecareforadults.nhs.uk

National Audit Office
Website: www.nao.org.uk/
Report By The Comptroller And Auditor General
HC 1043 Session 2007-2008, 26 November 2008

Alzheimer's Society
Website: www.alzheimers.org.uk

Bupa Care Homes
Have over 300 care homes throughout the UK, offering a range of specialist services for residents funded privately, by Social Services or by the NHS.
Website: www.Bupacarehomes.co.uk

CHAPTER 5

FUNERALS AND MOURNING

Planning your own funeral or helping someone to plan theirs in advance is not easy. However, when the end of life occurs it does help to ease the emotional and financial strain on friends, family and loved ones at a very difficult time if wishes are known beforehand. In fact some people may find that planning their funeral brings comfort and reassurance. Even when plans have been made, death comes as a shock and we may find it difficult to think clearly about what needs to be done. In this chapter we discuss what happens after someone dies and what arrangements need to be made. Not everyone wants a conventional funeral and different alternatives are discussed. Some requirements, such as registering a death, are a matter of law and have to be done; others are a matter of personal desire and religious, family or other convention, and these are the matters which may cause the most stress and difficulty.

When someone dies, a doctor will issue a 'cause of death certificate' (generally referred to as a 'death certificate') unless a post mortem is required because the doctor is not happy that the cause of death is clear. (Following a post mortem the coroner will issue an E certificate (which is for cremation) or a notification for burial.) The death certificate states the cause of death. If you have been expecting death to occur and have been involved in planning for the end of life, then the doctor will normally have been in regular attendance and there should be no difficulty about the issue of the death certificate. Therefore, when someone dies at home you should contact the family doctor or whichever doctor has been attending. They will call round at the house and will normally issue the death certificate then. Sometimes they will return to the surgery to write the certificate and you may be asked to call round later to collect it.

If someone dies in a hospital or hospice, or at a nursing/care home, the staff there will make the necessary arrangements for a doctor to issue the death certificate and will advise you about collection arrangements. They will also liaise with the funeral directors about collection of the deceased and/or removal to a chapel of rest.

If the wish is for a cremation then you should let the doctor, hospital or care home know about this, as additional papers have to be prepared and knowing about this in advance may save possible delays.

If the person who has died has made no funeral arrangements in advance, nor left any information about what they would like, then decisions fall to the nearest relatives. Although by law the executor of a Will is responsible for arranging (and arranging payment for) the funeral, in practice this is often a collaborative effort, with many of those nearest to the deceased being involved.

Immediately after death most people rush to telephone a funeral director, partly because there is a natural need to take some action and partly because they do not know what else they should do. (But see the note on different cultures below.) If the person has died at home then the doctor will usually advise you to call the funeral director straight away. However, you do not need to do this in a hurry. You can wait a while and spend some quiet time with the person who has died, consider what you would like to do and think about any wishes they might have expressed about their funeral (even if these were not actually formally recorded). Generally, once they have been contacted the funeral directors will arrive as soon as possible and will remove the body of the deceased to their premises. They will invite you to call there at your convenience to make follow-up arrangements.

In some cultures and for people with certain religious beliefs, specific rituals have to be carried out immediately after death. Some orthodox religions will not allow the services of a funeral director to be used at all and all arrangements have to be carried out through the local place of worship (for example, the mosque or synagogue).

It is actually wise to delay attending at the funeral directors until you have had time to think about the deceased's wishes, your own wishes and the views and desires of other relatives and close friends. You can write down any ideas or wishes that you or others have and begin to put together a 'funeral plan' in your own mind so that when you do eventually go to make the arrangements you will not feel rushed or persuaded into anything that you later regret. Although it is a comfort at this time to consider what the deceased would have wanted, in the absence of any expressed wishes you should not spend time worrying about this or feeling guilty if you are unsure of what those wishes might have been. Nor should you feel under any obligation to take everyone's ideas into account (for example, if a relative insists on a specific reading or hymn as being particularly appropriate). Remember that this is a stressful time for everyone concerned and a period of calm and reflection will be beneficial. You can eventually go to make arrangements with an outline plan in mind.

Funeral directors are experienced at caring for the deceased and making funeral arrangements. This is an obvious statement, but it is meant to assure you that the funeral director will be able to help you with whatever arrangements you wish to make. Even if your wishes are unusual or complicated, the funeral director will normally be able either to accommodate them or to help you to make whatever arrangements are necessary.

It is important at this point to make an assurance with regard to costs. The costs of the funeral are supposed to be borne by the 'estate' (the money and valuables that have been left after death) of the deceased. Funerals are usually expensive; some might consider them unnecessarily so. But help is obtainable if required. Sources of information about this are given in the reference section.

As a general rule you will initially have a fairly lengthy meeting with a representative of the funeral directors and at this meeting most arrangements will be discussed, such as the date of the funeral and/or cremation, whether you require a church service, flowers, funeral notices and so on as well as details such as the make and style of the funeral casket (coffin) and what vehicles will be used at the funeral. Remember that many of these arrangements can still be changed later. Generally anything can be changed at any time, except on the day itself. You may be astonished at the details which the funeral director will take care of and the questions you will be asked. If you have not yet decided on some details and need time to consider them, do not let yourself be rushed into taking a decision. Many decisions can be delayed for a few days.

> *Of course I had no idea how complicated it was to arrange a funeral. We were all completely numbed by the shock and to be honest we were just glad that someone took the arrangements off our shoulders. Even deciding the order of service for the funeral was like an insurmountable problem because we were so stressed.*

However, you do not have to use the services of a funeral director. Many people do not realise that there is no legal reason to do so and that they can simply organise a funeral themselves. The idea of arranging a funeral can be daunting and perhaps you may not have contemplated it. However, you can find out all that you need to do and this may be your preferred option. Firstly, a self-organised funeral can work out very much cheaper and can sometimes assist people to come to terms with their loss. A very personal ceremony can be created and family and friends asked to contribute their ideas or their service in some capacity. Some people might feel this is one final and very loving thing they can do.

There are very few regulations covering the disposal of a body in the UK. You must undertake either to bury or to cremate it, and you must have a death certificate signed by a doctor and a Certificate for Burial or Cremation from the Registrar of Deaths. This last document is very important, and most hospitals and mortuaries will not release the body until they've seen it.

Later on in this chapter are some ideas to help anyone who wishes to arrange an alternative funeral.

Sources of advice

Some undertakers offer advice for DIY funerals, although they will make a charge for this. If you are planning the burial or cremation to take place at a local authority cemetery or crematorium, their management can advise you on how to proceed. The Natural Death Centre (see page 101) is unique in providing the only independent funeral advice service in the UK.

A great deal of organisation is involved. For example, you will need to decide where the service is to take place (at a cemetery, crematorium chapel or at another religious or secular building). You will then need to book the time and place. You will need someone to officiate at the service. You will need to arrange the service itself (for example, if music is required you may need to book an organist or a choir). Transport for the coffin must also be organised and information given about flowers or charitable donations. If there is to be a burial you may have to organise the digging of the grave (and infilling afterwards) and you may even have to provide the rope for lowering the coffin.

Although a DIY funeral may be cheaper than that organised through a funeral director, you will still have to pay for the grave and the burial or the cremation. However, you can provide your own burial casket (coffin) and ask friends or family to be pall-bearers. Family and friends could make their own floral tributes (if you wish for flowers). Family and friends could also provide the singers and music if you wish for these.

The coffin

You can make or obtain a coffin and ask staff at the hospital or municipal mortuary to put the body into it. Some crematoria and cemeteries may accept bodies without coffins (you might prefer to use a shroud, for example), but do check with them first. The container should be clearly labelled with the person's name and date of death.

A casket or coffin is a shaped container for the body. Usually it has a separate lid, although in some countries a rectangular coffin is used with a hinged lid which is sometimes divided so only the upper part of a body may be revealed for a viewing. Funeral directors may be helpful if you ask them to conduct a funeral for which you supply your own coffin. Some may be prepared to sell you a coffin, if you intend to undertake the funeral organisation yourself. A few local authorities offer a direct coffin supply service. Coffins and caskets made from recycled wood, renewable forests, cardboard, bamboo or woven wicker have recently become available in response to demand from environmentally concerned people. The Natural Death Centre can advise on these.

If you wish, you can make your own funeral casket from whatever material you choose. However, in the case of a cremation the casket has to be a natural material and not highly lacquered because certain materials give off emissions that can set off the alarms in the crematorium and lacquer can cause a back flash in the cremator. It is best to get advice from the crematorium.

Transporting the body

You do not need to use a hearse. You can transport the coffin in any dignified vehicle, be it an estate car or a horse and carriage, as long as it's big enough. If you're considering a particularly unusual mode of transport, check with the cemetery or crematorium first.

The journey time between the starting point and the crematorium or cemetery is critical, and can vary with traffic conditions at different times of day. Professional drivers will know the best routes and times, but if you're doing it yourself it's a good idea to check the route in advance.

Four pall-bearers are usually enough, unless the coffin/casket is large or of an unusual shape. You may choose to ask specific family members or friends to undertake this task. Often coffin handles are not strong enough to support the weight and so hands should be placed beneath the coffin to lift and carry it. Pall bearers do not need to be male, although strength to carry the weight is a consideration.

Even if you are planning to use the services of a funeral director, the actual funeral service will most probably be planned by the family closest to the deceased. Most people consider this event to be very important and are determined to do the best they can. Such thoughts are natural and even praiseworthy, but if you are involved in the arrangements and planning of the funeral do not allow a determination to 'get it right' or even to 'do what he/she (the deceased) would have wished' to blind you to practicalities or to cause you undue stress at what is already a difficult time. It might help to remember that, even if you have been left instructions, the funeral is part of the mourning ritual for those who are left behind. It is probably also worth remembering that you are unlikely to be able to please everybody.

> *Both his brothers and his sister were so certain that they alone knew what hymns my husband would have wanted and what readings would be 'best'. I found it hard to believe that they thought they knew him better than I did, and also that they were prepared to argue the toss without regard to my feelings.*

For ordinary practical matters you may find that the funeral director will be the best person to advise you. For example, you will have to decide whether you wish for one or more funeral cars to make a 'cortege' procession from your home to the place where the service is to be held. There are conventions about who travels in the cars immediately behind the hearse (usually the spouse, children and brothers/sisters of the deceased) and it may help to observe such conventions to avoid arguments amongst the family. Similarly, if you are planning to have floral tributes the funeral directors will be able to help and advise as to what will be appropriate and how these can be displayed. You do not have to follow convention in these or any other matters, but it may ease the burden and stress of the arrangements to do so.

If you are planning a Christian religious service, the funeral director can contact the priest, vicar or minister on your behalf to book the date for the funeral. However, you may prefer to do this yourself. In any case, the minister concerned will wish to have a private discussion with the family concerning the order of service. Here again you might find it helpful (if you have not been given any indication of the wishes of the deceased) to ask the minister's advice. They will know of suitable readings and appropriate hymns that you might use. However, if you or the close family have ideas, by all means put them forward. It is quite common these days to have non-religious songs and secular readings, for example a poem, even at a Christian religious service. The minister will also be able to guide you about the length of the service and the number of hymns/songs and readings that can be fitted in.

If you are planning a religious funeral of any non-Christian faith, then again, usually the funeral director will be able to help. A majority of funeral directors are able to accommodate the diverse requirements of the different religions and will have contact with the relevant faith ministers.

If you do not wish for a religious service at all you can still plan a service that suits you. Some people like to call it a 'Celebration of the life of...' or something similar. In this case you may like to ask a member of the family to lead the ceremony, or a close friend of the deceased. Again, you can, if you wish, ask the funeral director to help you. They would normally use a humanist celebrant to take the service and there would be a charge. A non-religious service might take the form of favourite songs and music, poems or other readings and individual 're-membrances' (sometimes called eulogies) by different friends and family. You could display photographs or pictures and other memoranda at the same time.

> *When Katherine died, we applied for permission to bury her in the bluebell wood that was in the grounds of our house. She had stated that she wanted to be buried in a biodegradable casket. We held the service in the local parish church and the vicar allowed us to do more or less what we wanted providing he could say a short prayer. We had very calming classical music playing in the background as everyone entered the church. After some of Katherine's friends had spoken, we made a procession that led down a grassy slope from the church to the burial ground. The casket was carried by funeral directors, and her friends and family followed it. We all made a huge circle around the grave and everyone was given petals and flowers, which we each in turn tossed onto the grave. While we were doing that, there were some singers, I think from Africa, who sang native burial songs. It was very moving and without doubt a ceremony that none of us will ever forget.*

Most people have heard of the terms 'wake' or 'funeral meats' and understand that some sort of gathering with refreshments is expected after the funeral. It is really very important to have such a gathering and since some people may have travelled a long way to attend, food and drink are an important element. Ideally it should be near the burial grounds or near the home of the person who died. This gathering allows time for the mourners to meet each other, to reminiscence about the person who has died and to express their condolences to the family left behind. There are many times when mourners who have heard each other's names mentioned for many years are finally actually introduced and meet each other at the funeral. If you wish, the gathering and refreshments can be arranged by the funeral director.

I met Claire's sister at Claire's funeral. It was really bizarre because I had heard details of her life through Claire for the past 30 years and yet it took a funeral for me to finally meet her face to face. It turned out that she knew as much about my life as I knew about hers, which made us both smile and we have stayed in touch, more to comfort each other really, but it seemed quite paradoxical that our meeting took place under those circumstances.

These post-funeral gatherings are an important part of the grieving process, when you can continue to talk about the deceased, to share memories and to share sorrow, and it also gives the immediate family an opportunity to communicate their pain with others who also are feeling the loss.

It is not important whether the after-funeral social is held at home, at a pub or at a local hotel, but it is preferable that there be a specially designated area for the mourners to sit rather than be part of a larger anonymous gathering. It is also a good idea if someone is designated as organiser or 'master of ceremony'. This should be someone other than the chief mourners or immediate family. This organiser can make sure that everyone is welcomed, that the family have a chance to speak to all who have called to pay their respects, and, very importantly, they can ensure that disagreements don't turn into major hostilities, that old quarrels are not resurrected and that the immediate family are not more upset than necessary. Feelings run very high at this emotional time and it is not unknown for major feuds to have their beginnings in a perceived slight at the funeral ('Auntie Em should have gone in the front car') or for past disagreements to be raked over and highlighted ('You never liked him anyway!').

It is after the funeral and the funeral tea that the people closest to the deceased may really start the grieving process. Some people have mentioned that the period after the funeral is 'when the caravans have left' as though there was so much activity around the period between the death and the funeral that there wasn't much time to think, and when it is over there is silence. Everyone has gone home. The drama is over and what is left is the reality of life without the deceased.

Many say that initially the pain of loss is masked by the activity and the ensuing outpouring of emotion and support, but then after the funeral you are left alone with your grief. The pain is multifaceted, every facet reflecting the loss of the different roles the person filled. This may be a very good opportunity for someone to organise and make arrangements so that the family members of the deceased continue to have ongoing support. Although there are some people who prefer to be left alone, a majority feel very isolated after the funeral, and it is a very good idea if some caring person can make an informal rota for those who live nearby to visit, and those who live far away to phone regularly.

Those who were not so close to the person who died can get on with their lives after the funeral but those who were close will be struggling with facing the future and your ongoing concern and support will be very valuable.

My husband died very suddenly. He went into hospital for a minor operation and caught one of the super bugs that were doing the rounds at the time and he died within 48 hours of us realising that there was something seriously wrong with him. The shock waves were terrible: he was 40 and he was very athletic so there was a huge amount of emotional drama leading up to the funeral. His family and many childhood friends came from abroad for it and it was a very, very emotional time. My son was only six at the time, and he and I were in complete shock. It wasn't until everyone had left, gone back to their respective countries, that the reality started to dawn on us that my husband was not in fact coming back. By that time everyone else had started to get on with their lives. I needed the family

> *to come at that time, not immediately after his death, but a few months later when I was realising the enormity of the event.*

It may be helpful to remind yourself that the funeral is just a passage along the way in adjusting to life without the person who has died. It is not an end in itself. If we do not get things quite 'right', those who have passed away would not condemn us for they would know that we had done the best that we could and those on earth who love us will forgive us anyway. If you really feel upset, that you did not plan the ceremony 'just as it should have been' you can consider the possibility of a memorial service at a later date. Some people have a ceremony of 'scattering the ashes' many months later when everyone is less grief stricken and it is possible to remember the happy times with affection. Or perhaps you can simply decide that you did the best you could in the worst of circumstances and put your regrets behind you.

The journey of grief is a solitary one. Although we have no choice but to walk it alone, this is a period of time in our lives when we need to access as much support from the community as possible, and yet paradoxically at this time our emotional energy is at its lowest, and we are least able to reach out and ask for the help that we so badly need.

In the past someone who was 'in mourning' was easily recognised, which enabled others to treat them with extra consideration and gentleness at this time. The first recorded signs of mourning date from as far back as the ancient biblical civilisations. There are examples in the Old Testament of the ancient Hebrews placing dust or earth on their heads as a sign of grief and distress.

Sackcloth and ashes are mentioned several times in the Bible as an external symbol of repentance and grief. In biblical times the bereaved person would wear sackcloth and sit in dust and ashes and put ashes on their forehead as a sign of mourning. In some cultures this has survived to this day. One theory for this is that the biblical society was one that relied on wood fires for both their heating and cooking needs, which meant that keeping the fire under control was a major and crucial housekeeping task. If someone was grieving they didn't always have the energy to 'keep the fire burning'. If someone came to pay their respects they might say, 'Did you know you have ashes on your face?' So ashes became a sign of mourning. Rending garments as a sign of grief is also mentioned in ancient texts.

There is a tradition in many cultures of wearing a specific colour as a sign of mourning. The colour chosen is often black, but white is considered appropriate in many cultures. This tradition was common in western society during the past two centuries, with the mourner wearing dark or black clothes for some time after a death. In Victorian times this was taken to considerable excess and a widow would wear deepest black and not leave the house for several weeks. She would only appear in public heavily veiled and might wear a particular form of headdress – the 'widow's cap'. Men too wore unrelieved black. Mourning was only gradually 'lightened' over a period of months so that one might slowly begin to wear grey or very sober colours. The final 'stage' in this mourning was the wearing of black gloves for women and a black tie or black mourning armband worn on the left arm between the shoulder and elbow for men. The black armband has traditionally been recognised as a symbol of mourning and was a signal to the community that the wearer had been bereaved.

Along with many other mourning customs, this tradition has fallen into disuse in the western world, although it does still remain in many cultures and on some public occasions in the West – for example, where the wearer of a black armband wishes to identify with the commemoration of a comrade or team member who has died. But generally in western countries the wearing of black – even sometimes to the funeral itself – is now considered old-fashioned and the custom has fallen into disuse. There is an unfortunate consequence to this.

The end of the tradition of wearing black, or a black armband, has meant that those in mourning no longer have an external sign of their internal emotional state. There is no obvious way for their grief to be announced to those who do not know them and an unhappy mourner is more likely to be considered as 'having got out of bed on the wrong side' than to be grieving.

> *I own a craft shop and when I returned from my mother's funeral in the States the last thing I felt like was being pleasant and making superficial chit chat to my customers. I wished there were an external symbol to show my clients that I was in mourning, because of course I did not feel comfortable about telling them that I was grieving for my mother.*

> *I remember taking my two children (aged seven and three) shopping a couple of weeks after my husband had died. My son asked if we could buy ice-cream and when I agreed he whooped with pleasure. I vividly recall the disgusted look on the face of the elderly lady next to us. I really wanted to say, 'Look, his Dad has just died. Thank goodness he can feel some pleasure in a small thing – and I can be glad that he is happy for a few minutes.' Maybe if we had all been in mourning clothes she would have been less ready to condemn.*

It is for this reason that we strongly advocate the return of an external symbol to allow the mourner to make known that they have suffered a loss without having to make an embarrassing announcement that most would shy away from doing. We suggest the symbol of the leaf, which has no religious or cultural significance, and yet, at the same time, holds a universal symbolic significance (relating to the tree of life, the eternal changing of the seasons, nature, varying seasonal colours, falling autumnal and winter leaves, absorption back to the soil signifying the circle of life, etc). It has an easily recognisable connection to nature, the ultimate circle of life. We choose a deep purple colour to distinguish it from a leaf worn as a decorative brooch.

It represents the seasons of autumn or winter, a leaf that has lived through the different cycles of life and no longer has the strength to stay attached to the tree. It can be worn for as long or short a time as required. There is no time limit on grief, nor is there a time limit on the process of grieving.

A leaf can be worn on days when the mourner is feeling particularly sensitive, no matter how long since the death occurred. Or perhaps it might be worn on an important anniversary – for example, the anniversary of the death, much as in the United Kingdom we wear the poppy on Remembrance Sunday. On these occasions, no matter how much time has elapsed, one may be feeling particularly vulnerable and sad. Mother's Day or Father's Day may be a very painful reminder for some who have lost a parent, or a child, and perhaps wearing the symbol of mourning may offer a small protection from the celebrating multitudes around us.

> *Mother's Day is the worst day of the year for me. Not only did I lose my mother to cancer last year, but I lost my daughter five years ago. I do my very best to go abroad for that period of time because every card I see and every reminder feels like a knife through my heart. It seems that each occasion when the rest of the country is celebrating I just want to crawl into a hole and hide. I wish there were some external sign that would let people know that I am not only not celebrating, but in need of very careful handling!*

The leaf is also an unobtrusive sign. Someone who is in a senior or managerial position or involved in a work-related event and who is grieving may want others to know that they have suffered a loss without having to reveal verbally that this is so. So the leaf also sends a subtle message, and a leaf-shaped brooch or pin can be an inexpensive gift or symbol. When you see someone wearing the symbol of a leaf you will know that that person is grieving and, although asking for whom they are grieving may not be an appropriate question, a sympathetic look or a more sensitive way of communicating with them may go a long way to comforting the mourner and helping him or her to feel less alone.

The leaf symbol may also give an opportunity for connecting with others who have also suffered a recent loss or wish to support you in your journey. If someone comments on the brooch you can assist in perpetuating the symbol and play an active part in helping it to become an international symbol of grief.

We have designed a leaf 'pin' that is available on the website for this book. It would make an appropriate and thoughtful gift for someone who has been recently bereaved.

Further sources of help and information

The Natural Death Centre
Tel: 0871 288 2098
Website: www.naturaldeath.org.

British Humanist Association
Tel: 020 7079 3580
Website: www.humanism.org.uk

Funeral poems and readings and music
Website: www.rememberlife.com
Website: www.funeral-music.co.uk
Website: www.cofe.anglican.org

Arrangements following death and paying for funerals
Website: www.direct.gov.uk/en/Governmentcitizensandrights/Death

End of Life – The Essential Guide to Caring
Website: www.Endoflifebook.com

'The authors' end of life support organisation
Website: www.ELManagement.org

What to do when someone dies
Website: www.direct.gov.uk

Bereavement Advice Centre
Website: www.bereavementadvice.org/index.php

CHAPTER 6

END OF LIFE FOR PEOPLE WITH SEVERE MENTAL AND COGNITIVE IMPAIRMENT

If you are caring for someone at the end of their life who has a severe mental or cognitive impairment – for example, as a result of severe mental illness, learning disability or dementia – you will not be surprised to find that there is very little information published on palliative care needs in this area. Some of you will know from experience that mental health needs have always been your focal point when considering care.

This lack of information about the end of life probably comes to you hard on the heels of a lifetime of battling with health services to get equal health rights and the exhausting and endless fight to avoid being treated as second-class citizens, especially by some hospitals. Many difficulties and frustrations are faced by both formal and informal carers at a time when they most need to be supported by 'the system'.

Hospices and specialist palliative care services are geared towards people who are known to have a short life prognosis and since it is very complex to judge the prognosis of end-stage dementia, people suffering from it often do not receive palliative care. In fact they may be given care intended to prolong their life – for example, they may be tube-fed, resuscitated or given treatments which are uncomfortable, unpleasant and inappropriate.

Symptom-control occurs in the general population when patients communicate their need to health professionals. The loss of cognitive abilities makes pain assessment very complicated, as pain and distress may be hard to recognise in those who do not have conventional communication skills. There is evidence that pain assessment is inadequate and that these people's pain is being under-treated. Medical staff can feel that they lack the skills to work safely and effectively with people with such impairments and that expert care is needed to help manage medication and pain relief.

Although people with severe mental and cognitive impairment have difficulty in communicating effectively or in a way that is easily understandable, it is important for hospital and hospice staff to realise that a person who has these impairments and who is at the end of their life will have similar physical symptoms to other patients with the same illness, will most likely suffer similar pain and distress, and will also need support not only for symptom relief, but also psychological and spiritual support, as will their carers, both formal and informal.

Generally, society has a negative attitude towards people with any kind of mental health illness, which, combined with a lack of understanding, forces many of these people to be marginalised and their carers to come up time and time again against barriers to obtaining the physical care that they need. Often symptoms of serious illness (for example, cancer) are overlooked, especially if there is little obvious and visible sign. So when the symptoms do become visible, the illness is already at a late stage and more difficult to treat.

Even after a place has been found in a hospital or nursing home for end-of-life care, it is sometimes felt by carers and family that the nurses and other medical staff do not understand that the care-needs of their loved ones differ from those who have full cognitive ability.

> *Nurses don't take on board that he doesn't realise that he has to call when he is in pain.*

> *Because I'm used to caring for her I know that when she starts to wriggle she needs the toilet, but although I have told the nurses this they continue to ignore her needs and she spends hours in a wet bed.*

Some hospices and specialist palliative care services may become directly involved with people suffering from end-stage dementia, but usually only when there are complex needs and the prognosis is clear. However, in general they lack the skills and knowledge required in caring for the behavioural needs of these individuals. The hospice staff gain much satisfaction from the relationship with their patients, but this is not entirely applicable to people with dementia or severe mental illness; they may be unaware that they are at the end of their lives and their behaviour may be viewed as challenging to the staff, who will probably not have been trained in end-of-life dementia care.

> *My mother was admitted to hospital after a fall. When I visited her the staff continually complained about her 'hostility' and 'aggression' even though I had explained to them that she had quite advanced dementia. What was I supposed to do about it? Their continual complaints made me feel very uncomfortable and certainly did nothing to aid my mother's recovery.*

Carers of people with advanced dementia have additional stress in not knowing the prognosis of the person's illness and not being able to prepare themselves for an unpredictable life expectancy. Sometimes the fact that the patient no longer recognises the carer and is unable to share important memories or conversations is an added frustration and cause of stress. Some carers' need for respite is great but so is the need to have continuity of care and these two needs are not compatible.

Perhaps with additional training hospital staff could be educated in the particular needs of those with severe mental and cognitive impairment and on admission carers could be consulted about the best methods of communicating and would be involved in care and in decision-making. However, until that happens, if you are the carer of someone with a severe cognitive or mental impairment, there are things that you can do to make a stay in hospital or nursing home a better experience.

Do not put off visiting because it is so stressful. In particular, do not allow the staff to put you off visiting 'because he is so much more settled when you visit less often'. Your visits are important for two reasons. Firstly, because you will be missed by the person you care for, and secondly, because you can help greatly to improve the quality of care which is being given. Any collaboration between you and the professional care staff can only be to the benefit of the person you are all caring for.

It is a mistake to believe that because someone is unable to articulate the fact that they miss you they do not feel sad at your absence. The person you care for knows that their familiar carer is not with them. Often you will be told things such as: 'He doesn't even know who you are', or 'When you are not there she is perfectly happy'. Such statements may be intended to reassure you. However, we can never know for sure that someone does not know who we are. Someone with dementia may no longer recognise the relationship between you, may be unable to call you by name, but they will almost certainly still realise that you are someone with whom they associate reassuring and comfortable feelings. They may recognise that you are someone who made them feel safe in an alarmingly confusing world. In a similar way, no stranger can gauge the truth about someone else's emotional state. A patient who is quiet and doesn't make a nuisance of themselves may be designated as 'quite comfortable and happy', but you may recognise that they could be depressed, withdrawn and apathetic. In short, your regular attendance is crucial.

Remember, you know the person best. You are best able to interpret his or her moods and needs. You are the one who can explain to nursing staff what signs he/she makes when in pain or in need of the toilet, why he/she will be agitated if the bed is not made in a certain way, or how best to help him/her to eat the food needed. Even if you feel that some nursing staff do not listen or do not act on your information, you can at least try to do your best for the one you care for. In the worst case scenario, you can do practical things to help him/her – change the bed sheets; help to make sure he/she is clean; if he/she is able, help him/her to leave the bed and sit in a chair; bring his/her favourite flowers; assist with drinking and eating. You can take him/her out of the ward or room for a change of scene. You can speak on his/her behalf to the medical staff and ask about treatment and prognosis. Above all, you can talk to him/her, listen, give hugs, be a familiar sight in a strange and confusing situation. If you do not visit you will not be able to do these crucial tasks.

It is important to do your best to maintain pleasant relationships with the staff. It is true that you have handed over the daily care of the person you have been looking after to others. This can make you feel very defensive and guilty, but remember that the person you have been caring for is in hospital or nursing home because this is where they can receive the care they need at the end of life. Try to remember that, as has been said before, most medical staff mean well and enjoy caring for others and they also have the medical and professional expertise and skills which informal carers do not have. A majority of nursing staff want to do a good job and to make those they care for feel comfortable and secure. Many succeed in doing so.

Although this is not always easy, try to maintain a composed manner during your visits so that the person you care for is able to associate your presence with a feeling of calmness and security. It is exceedingly helpful if there are others who are familiar to the person in hospital and who can share the burden of visiting to give you some respite.

When a member of our church congregation went into hospital with her last illness we organised a rota so that she always had a visitor who was well known to her and her husband had some

> *respite. Those of us who did not know her so well got together*
> *and fixed up to make meals for her husband and two children,*
> *to take the children out sometimes and to organise the shopping*
> *and laundry for the family. We didn't all feel able to be at her*
> *bedside, but we felt we could at least do something to help.*

Dying at home is the wish of the majority of people facing the end of their life and many problems can be managed at home with specialist help (such as Twilight nurses, or Marie Curie nurses in the case of cancer care). Unfortunately, as the health of the person at the end of life deteriorates, so does the ability (or sometimes the desire) of the family or staff of the care home to take care of them, so an ambulance is called. In a very few care homes the decision is made fairly early on that transfer to hospital for the final days should be avoided unless absolutely necessary, and in these cases all possible steps are taken to keep the resident in the home. In some cases the family and staff agree that the resident remains in the home and they take care of them as best they can, endorsing the principle that this is their home and they have a right, if they so choose, to die there. (See 'Advance Statements' in chapter 1 on Practical issues.)

Some care workers are unwilling to undertake end-of-life care, feeling that they don't have the necessary nursing skills or experience. Many also have emotional difficulty with working in the area of end-of-life and feel that they took a job as a care worker and not an 'end of care' worker. It can also be very sad and very stressful to manage end-of-life care on a continual basis, and not surprisingly many care workers, especially those who lack any proper training in this area, find they cannot accept the sadness and stress after a period of time.

What follows is the story of one home in Surrey that, with the agreement of family and social workers, made the decision that one of their long-term residents who was suffering from both Down's syndrome and Alzheimer's disease would be allowed to remain in the home where he had lived for 12 years, until he died.

Alzheimer's is very common in people with a learning disability. The two conditions have a chromosome in common (chromosome 21). This connection was not really relevant until recently because the life expectancy of people with Down's syndrome was often no longer than 20 years. Now, because their life expectancy is longer, Alzheimer's disease is becoming more and more prevalent in learning disability homes, with approximately 54 per cent of over 60s showing signs.

Jonathan's story is an example of exceptional and perhaps unusual end-of-life care because the home really fought for him to have a quality end of life and remain where he wanted to be; the manager protected his right not to be resuscitated and to die, as he had lived, with dignity.

Jonathan Brown* from Farnham

Liz Hayes and Becky Morris (Manager and Deputy Manager):
'Jonathan had Down's syndrome and been living in the home (for learning disability) for 12 years when suddenly his behaviour changed. It seemed to us that in many ways he aged overnight. But he had a learning disability and people with a learning disability don't do normal things, so it is much harder to know if someone has the onset of dementia.

'His mother had recently died from Alzheimer's so initially the doctor diagnosed depression. Everyone agreed that he was depressed, but felt that something else was happening with him or maybe the depression had set off something else we still don't know about, and now never will. We tried him on anti-depressants but that didn't seem to help for long.

'But the most significant change was what happened to his total obsession with Manchester United. Every Saturday had been dedicated to the Manchester United game. He was completely fanatical. Then suddenly, almost overnight, his interest in that stopped. When we asked him which team they were playing he didn't know what we were talking about. It was Manchester United who? That was very significant to us.

* Not his real name.

'Finally we got the correct diagnosis and we asked Judy (one of the authors) to come and give us dementia training, which really helped because we then understood what was happening, how best to help him and we also understood that he was not going to get better. I think it was about a year from the diagnosis to the day he died. We wanted to keep him in the home because this was his home. The family also wanted him to stay and we told social services who were also in agreement. We redecorated his room and we asked if anyone wanted to back out of doing his care but no one did.

'Sometimes it felt as though we were going in between two parallel universes. In one room we had someone who was going to die, and in the other rooms we had residents who were expecting their dinner, and we went in and out of those two universes on a daily basis for several months.

'The staff didn't always agree on his care, which could be stressful at times. Some of the staff felt that it was OK to continue our normal lives in the home, making the usual noise and others felt that he should be in a quiet environment. Some of the staff felt he should get dressed and sit in his chair, others thought that if he wanted to stay in bed he should. There were also disagreements about his food and encouraging him to eat. But all the disagreement revolved around what we felt was the best for him; we all had his best interests at heart and all wanted the best possible end-of-life experience for him

'Towards the end – the last two weeks – he wouldn't eat and drink and some of the staff felt that he really should do so. I think each one of us subconsciously believed that for as long as he was eating and drinking we could delay his dying, but he didn't want to so in the end we all agreed to give him mouth care.

'One of the most stressful times was when the doctor said that he was going to die within the next few hours. We all piled in to his room and stayed there all night but it was another two weeks before he did die.

'We all spent many nights in his room. No one wanted him to be alone when he died but we couldn't be there 24 hours a day, seven days a week. Ultimately he died alone during the night when there were two girls on duty. The hardest thing was not being there when he died. I think again we each felt that we had let him down because we were not there for him at that moment. We were told that often people choose to die when they are alone.

'Strangely a few days before he died he said, "My mum said that she is coming to get me on Wednesday." He died on Wednesday.

'After he had died and before he left the home, some of us simply couldn't bear to go into his room and others felt very comfortable to go in and say a final goodbye. All the residents were allowed to go in and out of his room both while he was alive and also after he died. One of the residents who is Catholic wanted to see Jonathan after he died, and he went into the room and said a prayer for him.

'When he died I (the manager) phoned everyone on shift and sent texts to the staff on holiday at their request. Staff came in on their day off and we sat around talking. Clients didn't want to do activities that day. It was a strange sense of anti-climax and we all felt out on a limb. The family wanted him cremated but we knew he wanted to be buried in the local church. Jonathan had made that decision while he still had the capacity, so I had a bit of a struggle with the family, but he had written down what he wanted and I had to make sure that happened.

'After the funeral the family asked us to have a party and we had a service and the vicar came out with his guitar. Then Becky (the deputy manager) let off the biggest rocket that we could find – because we said we would see him off with a bang!

'We had a lot of training from Judy; she gave us end-of-life training and understanding of grief and loss and then came in for private conversations with the staff about their grief and they all had the opportunity to speak to Judy privately about how they felt, which was really important for all of us.

'His family gave us £2000. We cleared it with the Commission of Social Care Inspection and bought a huge TV for the lounge because Jonathan used to love watching TV. We will also buy something for the garden because he used to play hide and seek there. The family came as often as they wanted after he had died and we all went to his grave on the anniversary of his death.

'It was a privilege to have done it because when you've got through it, you know you can do it and come out the other end.'

Stacey Jackson:

'I came to work here three months before Jonathan died. Because I came late, I felt I was able to support everyone else. I wish I had been with him when he died. A few days after his death I went into the room next door and put a prayer book on the set of drawers and went out and when I came back it was gone. We searched everywhere and finally found it under the bed. I am sure that Jonathan moved it.'

Will Bosha:

'I saw it as a learning process and realised you have to take each day as it comes.

'At the very beginning of the process you don't think much about it. You think it is temporary and that he will bounce back so you are in denial – until you get to the point when you realise that in fact, there is no going back.

'Towards the end I used to give myself a target to make him eat two more spoons full. If he didn't want to eat, I couldn't say, 'Well, you wanted to eat yesterday' – basically you had to adapt, but emotionally as well you had to deal with him in the same way as you always had dealt with him, and not show him that you viewed him any differently.

'You had to show him the love you had always shown him. If you used to joke with him you still had to joke with him. One thing is that right up to when he died, he always used to smile, which was really nice.

'He had so many people around him who really loved him it made it a lot easier than it would have been otherwise. We all worked together and were dedicated to achieving the same outcome and Jonathan was always the main focus of the whole house.

'I didn't want to have the memory of him after he had died, so I didn't go into his room – I think this helped me to deal with it a lot better than if I had gone in after he had died.

'It was very helpful that there were so many of us all feeling the same way and we were there to support each other and we always had someone who understood what we were talking about. We can still; even today, talking about him to people who knew who he was really does help.'

Sean O'Donnell:

'It seemed to me that in the early stages of dementia he cut his meal sizes down and would only eat a small amount. Now I wonder if he knew he was becoming unwell. At some point you must realise that you are becoming forgetful. Sometimes he would be doing something like sweeping the floor and if you interrupted him he would forget what he was doing, and I think he knew that wasn't right.

'He went from a healthy size to quite skinny and that really upset me. Towards the end, every time I went into his room I wondered if I would find him dead. I think we all did. None of us wanted to be the one to find him dead, but we all wanted to be with him when he died.

'Terry (another resident) died very suddenly when I was abroad with some of the residents on holiday. I was Terry's key worker and I was only told when I got back. I took it very badly and couldn't forgive myself for not having been there for him when he died. We had all done the same things for Jonathan, which was helpful and we knew that we were all upset when he died and so I found it much easier to talk about it, but with Terry I felt that I was the only one feeling the way that I did.'

Pam Collaco:

'I come from India. In India we bring the body home and before sunset we have to bury or cremate it. We don't have funeral parlours. You go from the house to the burial grounds within 24 hours or there is a maximum wait of two or three days if there are family that need to come from abroad.

'We, the family, also bathe and dress the body, so for me death is nothing to be afraid of – I am very comfortable with death.

'People here in England die in the hospital and they go straight to the funeral parlour so there is no sense of closure. Then the mourners hang around for 10 days waiting for the funeral – not really having had closure and that's why I think people here grieve a lot longer. In India we have the body there in the house, and you get on with what you are doing – we keep the coffin open until you go to the graveyard so the visual effect gives you the ability to see the reality, which is that the person has died.

'At the end, when they are putting the body in the ground you are crying and beating your chest and when you come home there is a real sense of relief and closure. You can tell everyone is holding back during funerals here. There isn't the closure and it has an emotional snowball effect.

'When Jonathan died I felt I couldn't get through to people here in the home that it is alright to grieve or to show that they were grieving and I think they didn't know what to expect or how they would react and they suffered for a long time. I didn't because I sat in his room and sang songs and hymns because he was a churchgoer.

'I find English people don't like to talk about death and it's not that they are not feeling but they don't think it is alright to cry and be upset. And people here definitely grieve for longer. I wish people would talk more about it. I think it is because of the culture where they don't see their grandparents die or don't see dead people as part of the natural course of life.'

Karen Slade:
'I didn't want him to be alone when he died. That is the main thing that I remember.

'I remember thinking that we were looking after him the best we could but I think we felt we could have done more or if we had taken better care of him he wouldn't have gone downhill so quickly. We would try and do things to keep him alive like trying to encourage him to eat and drink, but it was a constant struggle. Of course, we knew what would happen if he didn't eat and drink but the fact was that if we kept offering him food we were distressing him.

'I think no matter how much I prepared myself it was still a shock when he died. Every day when my shift was over I went into the room to say goodbye to him. You can never say goodbye enough times. After he died when I went into the room to say goodbye it completely overwhelmed me. I knew it was the last time I would be able to say goodbye with him present.

'The house had revolved around that bedroom for so long it was hard to get back to normal. While he was alive it felt that the home had such a purpose. Then when he died, just having to revert back to the usual routine and get people up and dressed and just carry on – it was just weird and I found it very difficult. In a way I wanted to get back to normal but in another way I did just want to grieve. I thought, "How can you just go back to what you were doing?" – it felt superficial. I was annoyed at silly things like people needing underwear or toothpaste and I would think, "Is that really important right now?"

'I guess part of getting back into life is finding meaning in routine things.'

Author's note

During the dementia training in the above home, I noticed that the manager was distressed. I asked her whether she wanted us to take a break. She said no, she was upset because she felt that since they had not understood the nature of dementia they had been 'getting his care all wrong'. I asked her and the other care workers in the room if they loved Jonathan. They said they did. 'In which case,' I replied 'you have been getting it all right."

Further help and information

Publications

Addington Hall J. *Positive Partnerships: palliative care for adults with severe mental health problems*. National Council for Hospice & Specialist Palliative Care Services, 2000

Blackman N, Todd S. *Care for dying people with learning disabilities*. London, Worth Publishing, 2005.

Wilcock J, Froggatt K, Goodman C. End of life care. In: Downs M, Bowers B. *Excellence in Dementia Care*. Milton Keynes, Open University Press, 2008

Organisations to contact

Alzheimer's Society

Works to improve the quality of life of people affected by dementia and will support carers following the death of someone who had dementia as well as prior to death.

Telephone: 0845 300 0336

Website: www.alzheimers.org.uk

For their information on Down's syndrome and Alzheimer's disease www.alzheimers.org.uk/factsheet/430

Down's Syndrome Association

Aims to help people with Down's syndrome to live full and rewarding lives.

Telephone: 0845 230 0372

Website: www.downs-syndrome.org.uk

Foundation for People with Learning Disabilities

Works to promote the rights, quality of life and opportunities of people with learning disabilities and their families.

Different contact numbers through the website:

www.learningdisabilities.org.uk

Help the Hospices

Want the very best care for everyone facing the end of life.

Telephone: 020 7520 8200

Website: www.helpthehospices.org.uk

National Council for Hospice and Specialist Palliative Care Services

Website: www.HospiceCare.com

National Network for People with Learning Disabilities

Established by a small group of practitioners from learning disabilities and palliative care services.

Contact coordinator: Linda McEnhill – Linda.mcEnhill@st-nicholas-hospice.org.uk

The Regard Partnership

Operates homes and supported living services for people with learning difficulties, mental health problems or acquired brain injuries.

Website: www.regard.co.uk

CHAPTER 7

GRIEF

The journey through grief is one of life's most painful passages. You cannot escape from the journey and although others may travel the road with you, they cannot lift the burden you carry. Sometimes the pain can be so intense as to seem unbearable. You may feel that it is impossible to carry on and this intensity can lead some to people feeling that they are 'going mad'. If you feel this way, you are not going mad. What you are going through is entirely natural and normal.

Grief can also be a very selfish emotion. When we are in the midst of grieving we rarely recognise fully – though possibly we do theoretically – the pain that others are feeling. Even those close to us are not seen as feeling the pain as badly as we do ourselves. Our pain is often all we can experience. So you may find that you are quite unable to comfort others or even to acknowledge their own grief. One often hears well-meaning people say such things as, 'Well, at least she has her sons to help her,' or, 'Of course, they have other children and that will be a comfort.' The truth is that those around us, even if they grieve with us, do not alleviate our own burden. Indeed, sometimes it may increase the burden because we feel we have to 'be strong for others'.

> *After my sister committed suicide, someone introduced me to a woman at work whose mother had recently died, thinking that we might comfort one another. I just hated that woman! How could she be feeling as bad as I was? Her mother had lived a*

> *long and full life and she couldn't possibly feel the level of guilt that I did.*

Paradoxically, those who don't allow themselves to grieve because they don't want to 'let the side down', or because they are being 'strong' for others, will often find themselves totally unprepared for the grief when it does come.

> *When my fiancé died a few months before we were due to marry I didn't cry. I felt as though something inside of me was locked up and the pain was so overwhelming that I couldn't bear to face it. I pretended to myself and everyone around that I was coping and continued my life.*
>
> *I was very pretty and never short of invitations, and it wasn't long before I had another steady boyfriend. One evening we went to a restaurant. I asked for the menu and wondered why everyone was looking at me strangely. I suddenly realised I had tears streaming down my face and I simply couldn't stop them. I cried for days without stopping. My mother took me to the doctor; he called it reactive depression and gave me valium that made me feel worse. It was 30 years ago and I don't think we knew much about grief then; we certainly didn't talk about it. Then I started to feel dizzy all the time and sometimes had to excuse myself to go and lie on the floor of the bathroom at work. Looking back, I must have had some sort of breakdown, but it wasn't until several years later when I had therapy that I started to recover and was able to recognise that what had happened was probably due to not being able to grieve properly.*

I didn't grieve after my husband died suddenly from a heart at-tack. It was 25 years ago and there wasn't the knowledge that there is now. I got on with my life. I was very much part of a fashionable social scene – opening nights, cocktail parties and dinner parties almost every night. Grief didn't fit in at all well, especially at the age of 23. Who knew about grief? One evening my boss, forgetting some papers, returned to the office, opened the door and found me standing on the window ledge, 12 floors up. I had no recollection of climbing out of the window. Fortu-nately he had a lot of life experience and realised that this was a direct result of losing my husband and that I needed help. He made sure that I went to bereavement therapy, which probably saved my life.

Grieving successfully involves experiencing the pain. This means not trying to push it down, or push it away, or looking for shortcuts out of the pain experience. There is often a fear of feeling overwhelmed and losing control, so we may look for a way to avoid our feelings of grief, or we believe that if we bury ourselves in work or throw ourselves into family life and support everyone around us, we will be able to avoid the worst of it, as though taking a shortcut when seeing a traffic jam ahead. However, this may not be the best way to cope. You may find that when the shortcut ends you are back facing that same traffic jam but just a lit-tle further down the road. It may be that you will find out that the pain that you have been trying to avoid has been waiting for an opportunity or an (in) opportune moment to reveal itself.

An Israeli soldier had his legs blown off by a landmine. He was 18 and intended to be a professional basketball player. He was in hospital for a year and was the life and soul of the ward. He was the hero, always laughing and joking and flirting with the

> *nurses. His mother was an alcoholic and his father had vanished long before, so he had no one to support him. Ten years later he married and on his honeymoon he had a complete nervous breakdown and needed to be hospitalised. He remained in hospital for several months, working through his grief and recognising the devastating effect his injury had had on his life. It was as if the grief had waited until he was in a safe environment before it showed itself and allowed itself to be felt.*

All the emotions surrounding grief are intensely distressing and sometimes take on a physical element as though the emotional pain has a physical mirror. Elizabeth Kübler Ross was the first person to give the dying a voice and her first book, published in 1969, on *Death and Dying,* became an international best-seller (Simon & Schuster, reprinted 1997). She identified some of the signposts on grief's journey and recognised these when she was working with people who had a diagnosis of a terminal illness and were in fact grieving for the loss of their own lives. The stages that she identified in the 1970s are still an important aspect of the theory of grieving and are often quoted in relation to the grieving process for those left behind. They are: denial, anger, guilt, depression and acceptance. Since then there have been others who feel that her stages are too prescriptive and are sometimes used to make the grieving person feel as though he or she is not grieving 'correctly' – perhaps making him/her feel that he/she 'should have moved on to the next stage by now'.

W J Worden's *Four tasks of mourning* (Worden W J, 1983) is one of the most widely used theories among bereavement counselling professionals. Worden proposed that there are four 'tasks' and these are:

1. To accept the reality of the loss – We look and search for the person who died; we learn everything we can about him or her to understand that he or she is indeed really dead. We come to realise that we cannot just pick up a telephone or make a visit to share news about our lives.

2. To experience the pain of grief – There is so much pain during grieving, both physical and emotional. We may be very depressed, sad and tearful. It can be difficult to cope with everyday activities. We may want to keep busy constantly so that we don't think of our loved one's absence. We may feel angry or guilty. Often, during this time, we feel as if we are going mad.

3. To adjust to an environment in which the deceased is missing.

4. To integrate the deceased into a new future and to invest in new relationships and activities.

> *The worst thing was knowing, really knowing deep down, that there was no end. As my husband had been in the Forces we had often been separated and at first this felt just like another such separation – an overseas exercise where we could exchange letters and eventually experience a reunion. But then would come the realisation that my husband would never return from this 'exercise', that we would never be able to catch up on the past and bask in the reunion. It was almost impossible to come to terms with this and I frequently felt divorced from reality.*

The fact is that grief's journey is not a straight road. Grief has considerable individual, cultural, age and gender variables. It is never as ordered and predictable as the theories suggest. There is no 'one theory that fits all'. Nor should you ever allow anyone to make you feel that you *should be* anywhere other than the point that you have reached now. However, these theoretical stages and tasks can be a useful guide and comfort. Just knowing that you are not going mad and that there is a passage that will take you through the darkness into twilight, and then eventually into a place where there is some light, may be a help. There will be days when you feel you are going 10 steps backwards into disbelief and denial and other days when you may notice that it is a beautiful day, the sun is shining and you feel a sense of optimism. Everyone takes this journey in their own time and in their own way, and in this chapter we will try to give you some practical suggestions to take with you as well as some ideas on how to return to the world – when you are ready.

Grief is generally thought to be a universal reaction to loss and not purely a human experience. Katy Payne, author of *Silent thunder: in the presence of elephants*, states: 'What I have seen ... is that whenever an elephant comes to the bones of another elephant, it will stop and sniff and touch and roll over and fondle and carry and move and displace and pick up again and again those bones. How they respond when other animals die is with obvious symptoms of grief, despair and distress initially. They are called back and back to explore the corpse, called back by their own desires to return. And eventually when they leave the corpse there is obvious evidence of grieving.'

Jane Goodall, the expert on chimpanzees, saw mother chimpanzees carrying dead babies on more than one occasion, for up to a day, while the distinguished American naturalist George Schaller once saw a gorilla mother carry its dead infant for four days before finally abandoning the decaying corpse.

One 1996 study – the Companion Animal Mourning Project, conducted by the American Society for the Prevention of Cruelty to Animals – found that 36 per cent of dogs ate less than usual after the death of another canine companion, while 11 per cent stopped eating completely. Researchers also discovered that 36 per cent of dogs changed their vocalisation habits – whether by vocalising more or becoming quieter – while more than half became more affectionate and clingy with a caregiver, and two-thirds showed four or more behavioural changes. The study also included cats and found that in some instances, surviving cats even starved to death after the loss of an animal companion. A few years ago, in a facility in the US, two out of the centre's nine dolphins died within six months of each other. On both occasions, the other dolphins refused to eat for a period, would not play and would make distressed sounds, as if in mourning.

The above examples suggest that grief is not purely a human emotion. It appears to be a process during which we slowly let go of the individual we love and move into a place whereby we are able to continue life without them. Acceptance is very relative and often will never be complete, so each time you see the word acceptance, please don't throw the book across the room.

Grief is not only a reaction to death. Bereavement means 'to be deprived by death', but grief can occur when there is any loss (including home, country, relationship, etc). Grief can also occur when you realise that there is something you will never have. Perhaps when a parent dies it will not be for that parent that you grieve, but the parent that you never had and whom you now know you will never have. This is grief just the same, and you will see that the Kübler Ross stages also apply in such cases.

> *When my father died, I went into a deep depression. I had actually never had a good relationship with him so it seemed strange. My wife persuaded me to get help and it was only through therapy that I realised that my grief was not for the father that I had had, but for the father that I had never had and now never would.*

There are situations where we actually 'lose' the person we love even before their death. Our loved one may, for example, through injury be in a 'persistent vegetative state' for some time before death. We will have been unable to communicate with him/her even though his/her physical body is still present. The person has in a sense been 'dead' for some time even before actually dying. Even more harrowing are the cases where a loved one is being physically maintained with a ventilator and the decision must be made to remove life support.

When someone suffering from dementia dies it may also sometimes feel as though our loved one – the person we knew – 'died' long before.

The different factors that make us individuals also make each person's reaction to a dementing illness different, and it is these factors also that make the grieving process unique for each person. It is true to say that everyone reacts differently and that there is no typical reaction to grief. In cases like this, some or all of the stages of grief may be experienced before actual physical death takes place and then can be experienced again after the person dies.

When someone dies we experience shock. Even if the death has been expected or long anticipated, the event is a shock. You could say that the bereaved are 'in shock'. Shock and denial are a form of 'self defence for the mind'. The fact of death is so overwhelming that if this mechanism did not kick in perhaps our minds would be in danger of being permanently damaged. (This is especially true in cases of sudden and unexpected death, including suicide.) For example, someone who has just been told that their loved one has died may slip into 'automatic mode' and carry out routine tasks (putting the dustbins out, laying out the children's school clothing for the next day) even if these tasks are not essential. The feelings of shock may often preclude tears and other visible signs of grief, because the mind has not yet accepted any loss. Following hard on the heels of this feeling of shock comes (according to Elizabeth Kübler-Ross) denial. It is not uncommon for the bereaved to leave the bedroom of the deceased completely untouched as though keeping it ready for their return. A wife may refuse to dispose of her husband's clothing or a son insist on his mother's spectacles remaining in their 'usual' place. Incidentally, this form of denial also kicks in when we are given unexpected good news. Many of those who have won the lottery have stated that they simply could not believe it when they saw their numbers come up and asked several times for others to check it; it is the same self-defence mechanism preventing the mind from being overloaded. Feelings of denial may last a long time or they may recur long after those who are grieving think that they have reached the stage of acceptance.

Even three years after his death I sometimes pick up a family photograph and see my husband smiling in the family group. And out of the blue I think, 'He can't be dead. It isn't possible.

> *There he is ... he can't have ceased to exist.' It isn't sensible and
> I know this but I can't stop the feeling arising.*

Sometimes people claim to 'see' the person who has died, perhaps sitting in their favourite armchair or walking across the street towards them. These occurrences are not necessarily part of the process of denial. It is thought that such 'visions' happen because the brain is so used to seeing, for example, the person in the armchair, that it 'inserts' the vision where it expects it to be. Do not be alarmed if you experience these 'visions'. You are not going mad. They are very common and some people even find them comforting. There are other possible explanations of course – arguments for and against life after death still rage on – and there are many different books that cover these fascinating theories.

Anger is a very normal and healthy reaction. The anger is often directed at the person who has died as those left behind feel that they have been abandoned. ('How could you leave me?' 'How could he have been so stupid not to look when he crossed the road?') Sometimes anger may be directed at God for 'allowing this to happen'. Or the anger may be directed at the person who breaks the news: 'shooting the messenger'. Frequently the target of anger is the medical staff or health professionals involved, as those bereaved feel that their loved one died because of mistakes made by medical attendants: 'They could have done more'; 'They couldn't be bothered'. Sometimes people direct their feelings of anger into action. They may decide to sue the hospital, or perhaps more constructively, they set up a helpful website, or found a charity connected with the cause of death, or run a marathon to raise money for an existing charity. Although these actions may help to channel the anger, it is worth remembering that they are often born out of the anger which is a natural consequence of grief. It does not make constructive actions any less laudable, but it means that those who are grieving should be aware that there will come a stage when the anger has been 'worked through' and some other impetus may be required to reach the targeted end.

Few survivors escape some feeling of guilt. 'I should have done more', 'I should have known that he was ill' or 'I shouldn't have let her...' are words that are often heard. We rehearse over and over again all the things we could have done differently '... if only'. We may bargain with God: 'I promise I will [be a better person?] if you can only bring him back.' Or the guilt may take the form of brooding over the past and working out where 'everything went wrong': 'Maybe if I had only taken the job my father wanted me to take we would have got on better; now he is dead and it is too late to change into the person he wanted me to be.' Guilt may combine with anger. 'If I had persisted with my complaint about the treatment by the care home staff, then my mother wouldn't have died. It is all their fault – but also mine.')

If the person who has died was part of a difficult or destructive relationship it is very natural to feel relief after their death. However, many people often feel a sense of guilt that they are not sad or are still angry with the person even though they are no longer alive. Guilt is a normal emotion to experience when grieving. It is only when the guilt becomes overpowering and inescapable that we need to consider getting help in moving on.

When my partner died I had to speak to a young policeman. Poor chap, he really got it all wrong. He told me that only a few days earlier he had had to break the news of a death to a young mother, to which (suddenly coming to my senses) I replied, 'Oh my God, what do I tell the children?'

Back home I waited until the children woke in their own time. My four-year-old daughter immediately cried; my seven-year-old son was silent and went back to his bed. The night before his father had (unusually) shouted at him to 'Go to sleep'. Even after 15 years I've never asked my son whether he remembers their last words. I do.

At some stage the realisation hits that no matter what we say or do, the person that we love will not be coming back. This is often when depression overtakes the bereaved. Depression is the most inevitable emotion of grief. After the shock and denial have passed and the anger has been exhausted, sadness and even hopelessness may set in. For some, life really seems pointless, not worth living even. Some may find that they have little energy to do even the simplest daily chores. Some may go so far as to consider, or attempt, ending their own lives. Elderly people and those who suffer from depression at other times are thought to be most at risk of finding it really hard to move on from the depression that can be part of grief. Depression may come and go; it may return (like denial) suddenly, long after we believe we have 'got over' our loss. It is quite common for it to set in shortly after the first anniversary of the death. The generous support previously given by friends and family may begin to fall away around this time. Others may feel that now you have 'got through' all the anniversaries (birthday, Christmas, etc) in the first year you no longer need their support; you are 'through the worst'. Perhaps you have made life-style changes in the wake of the death (incidentally not a good idea) and now find yourself rootless or feeling bereft of your support network. You should not fear this depression. It is a natural part of your grief. In almost every case you will get through it. If, however, you find the depression seems to take over, if your family and friends are indicating that they are concerned about the length of time it has lasted, if you can really see no 'light at the end of the tunnel', you should seek medical help.

Grief is a process that has a start date, but has no expiry date. Time alone will not heal grief. It is a natural process and will not be helped by blocking emotions and refusing to allow them to surface or attempting to drown them out through alcohol or misuse of medication. Eventually you will find the ability to accept life without the person who has died. Accepting does not mean forgetting, but the constant wish for things to be as they once were can be replaced by a search for new relationships and new activities. A sense of longing may re-surface from time to time for years and this should be expected and even anticipated, especially whenever there is an anniversary or an occasion where the deceased was always present. But not all sensitive memories can be anticipated, and it can be the unforeseen link that can cause the most painful recollection and bring back the sharpest sting.

Tears are nature's healers. Not everyone has the ability to cry freely and those who are able to do so should treat this ability as a gift. It may not always be appropriate to break down in tears, but it is very much recommended that if you feel a need to cry, you excuse yourself and find a quiet place to do so; the benefits far outweigh the embarrassment of having a red nose and streaked cheeks. Having an emergency make-up kit in your handbag is useful for women who are going through bereavement. According to biochemist William Frey (Frey, 1977) emotional tears have a different content from, for example, 'crocodile tears', or tears shed whilst peeling onions. Emotional tears contain ACTH (adrenocorticotrophic hormone), which is a hormone associated with high blood pressure, heart problems, peptic ulcers and other physical conditions closely related to stress. It seems the act of crying eliminates these compounds, and causes stress levels to plummet.

It may be that the person who has died is someone with whom you had a difficult or painful relationship. Death does not mean that the conflicting feelings die with the person. Not everyone is loved and not everyone's life is one that is mourned. It is an aspect of the way some may romanticise the end of life, expecting it to be the last chapter in a drama. Sometimes it isn't. Sometimes it is the last act in a long and painful relationship. The death of someone with whom you had a difficult or destructive relationship can complicate grief, mainly because you still have all the angry emotions you had when that person was alive, but without anyone at whom to direct them.

Another complication when such a person dies is that you may indeed grieve for them, but your grief may not be recognised by your environment. People will assume that because your relationship was difficult, and maybe stormy, you do not feel the loss of it.

Any circumstance that causes a lack of support from the environment will complicate grief. Another example of grief not being recognised is that arising following an illicit and secret association that may have continued for many years. In a case like this, when one of the partners dies, it is impossible for the other to start to talk to their friends about the relationship.

We had been lovers for 43 years. He had made sure that a close friend of his would tell me when he died. So, I knew. But I could not attend the funeral, couldn't tell anyone except my closest family. Nor could I express my grief in any external way. I couldn't tell my work colleagues. The separation from most forms of natural support – the friendly understanding that those in a conventional relationship have – was the worst thing.

Sometimes a similar situation arises when a partner from a same-sex relationship dies. Your friends may believe that this was a platonic friendship or a flatmate and be unaware of the depth of the connection. This will leave you feeling isolated at a time when you most need support and is a circumstance in which it is very important to access professional help.

Any bereavement through suicide has deep complications for those left behind. The initial shock and disbelief can be very intense, especially because of the element of choice that is involved. There is often an inability to understand why the person took their own life, which is combined with an almost inevitable feeling of guilt and self-blame that is much greater in cases of suicide than in other causes of bereavement. There can also be a real sense of rejection through the person choosing to take his or her own life. These complications can be exacerbated by the attitude of those around the bereaved, who may feel embarrassed and uneasy about the way in which that person died and will leave them feeling even more intensely isolated. It is best to treat the bereaved in the same way that you would treat any other person who has suffered a loss.

When people are coming out of the worst of their grief they may need help in returning to 'life' – returning to the world. Those who have family or friends to assist and support them are fortunate, but there are many who do not have a good external support system. As you, the bereaved, progress through this journey, it is important that you do what you may least feel like doing, and that is to get out of your home. That is never more important than when the difficult and potentially destructive depressive stage occurs. Taking up the reins of your old life, or setting out to create a new life, is an important part of recovery. It does not mean that you are showing a lack of respect for your loss or the impact it has had on your life. Many people find that they can resume a 'normal' life relatively easily. This is often true if you have children or other dependants who need you and who can give you a reason to live. However, just as many people find this 'resumption of life' incredibly difficult.

Many people find that their work helps them to adjust. This may be especially true if your work involves any form of caring. When paid carers – whose salary is generally pitiful, compared to their responsibilities – talk about their jobs, what often shines through is their commitment and how rewarding they find it despite low salaries and low esteem by the general public. Any absorbing job is an advantage when trying to fill the gap which may be left by the death of someone close to you. A worthwhile and absorbing job fills time; gives a reason to get up in the morning; and often gives something to occupy the mind which might otherwise be consumed with destructive feelings of guilt or depression.

Not everyone has children dependent upon them, or an absorbing job to help them 'back into the world'. If your life seems empty, you could consider doing some voluntary work. Although it sounds like a cliché, volunteering is a win-win situation. If you work, you have the advantage of being forced to leave the house to go to your workplace, but if you are not working or have a lot of spare time on your hands, volunteering, even on a part-time basis, will pay dividends. Not only will you be contributing, but you will be interacting with other people, which is a vital aspect of good mental health, and you may find there will be some able to empathise with your circumstances. Human beings are cleverly wired to get enormous emotional benefits from helping others. One of the volunteers' best-kept secrets is they get much more out of volunteering than they put in. There are many areas where volunteers are needed. It is worth spending a little time working out what will interest you most, but do not let the researching become such a project that it prevents you from 'doing'. Not all volunteering requires a huge commitment or a lot of planning. For example, you could offer to help in a charity shop, or you could lend a hand with your child's cub-scout or brownie pack, or you could volunteer to help serve in the local hospital coffee shop. (Many are completely staffed by volunteers.)

If you are reluctant to make a long-term or regular commitment, there are still many ways you can volunteer and get out of the house. You could offer to help at a church bazaar, collect for charity during an awareness week, or perhaps even offer to help your local political party with canvassing at election time. Many people find great comfort and support in taking part in charity events for a charity which has some connection with the person they have lost. If you do not know how to get started, then there are websites which can point you in the right direction. There are also charities (see pages 134 and 135) which match those wishing to volunteer with organisations needing help.

Many who are grieving find that owning a pet can be a real life-line. There are rescue pets of varying ages and sizes with numerous built-in benefits looking for a home, and their unconditional love will never be more welcome than at this time. Those who have adopted rescue pets have almost unanimously stated that they have received from them much more than they have given. One woman told me that her gentle, loving Schnauzer saved her from an attacker in the park, and another told me, 'The rescue dog that I adopted gave me comfort during the long nights of grief that no human being would have been able to give.' If you are mobile, any dog will also force you to leave the solitude of your home to go 'walkies'. Any exercise is better than none, and exercise is a proven antidote to depression. Of course, owning a dog is a huge responsibility and although some people feel they need to have someone to care for, dogs are a tie. If you don't have a local dog walker or willing neighbour to help you out on days when you are away or unable to get out then perhaps adopting a cat would be a better idea. Alternatively, perhaps if you feel a dog would be too much of a tie you could offer to walk a neighbour or friend's dog on a regular basis or check with Cinnamon Trust, the charity that relies on volunteers to help the elderly, or those with a terminal illness, to take care of their pets. Most dog owners are happy to have their pet walked by a responsible person. Dog lovers are usually a friendly breed of human and often are more than happy to stop for a chat when meeting a likeminded soul. Pets have the added benefit of two empathetic ears that never grow tired of listening.

Often, bereavement brings a feeling that a dramatic change is needed in our life and surroundings. However, people grieving should not make any important decisions about a change of lifestyle and life events – particularly with regard to moving home – in the early months after bereavement. The first impulse often is to move – nearer relatives, to a smaller house, back 'home' and away from memories. Shortly after a bereavement is not the best time to make these decisions. Dr Shirley Holton, once medical adviser to a local housing authority, explained: 'I used to get a lot of applications from the recently bereaved for a change of their local authority house. My advice always was, "If you feel the same in six months, ask me again," and no-one ever did. I monitored this carefully so I could count the rate of re-application.'

Not surprisingly, being male is a factor that complicates grief. Men seem to have more difficulty sharing their emotions, so it is not surprising that more men than women use the Samaritans' service.

To sum up, perhaps it is almost enough just to remember that abnormal reactions and abnormal behaviour are normal during abnormal times. The period of grief is a difficult time and you get through it as best you can. Do not allow others to compound your grief by making you feel that what you are feeling, doing or saying is wrong.

References

Frey, W. *Crying: the mystery of tears*. Winston Press, Texas, 1977

Payne, K. *Silent thunder: in the presence of elephants*. Penguin, 1999

Kübler-Ross E. *On death and dying*. Simon & Schuster, reprinted 1997

Worden WJ. *Grief counselling, grief therapy*. Brunner-Routledge, 1983

Further sources of help and support

Alzheimer's Society

Supports carers following the death of someone who had dementia as well as prior to death.

Tel: 020 7423 3500 (or various local branches)

Website: www.alzheimers.org.uk

The Cinnamon Trust

Volunteers help the ill and elderly look after their pets.

Tel: 01736 757 900

Website: www.cinnamon.org.uk

Community Service Volunteers

Involves people in high quality volunteering and learning opportunities that enrich and tackle real need.

Tel: 0207 278 6601

Website: www.csv.org.uk

Compassionate Friends

For those unfortunate enough to have lost a child.

Tel: 0845 123 2340

Website: www.tcf.org.uk

Cruse

A bereavement charity that has branches all over the country. Free confidential help to bereaved people.

Tel: 0844 477 9400

Website: www.crusebereavementcare.org.uk

The Samaritans

The Samaritan service is available to all those in emotional distress 24 hours a day.

Tel: 08457 90 90 90

Website: www.samaritans.org

Suicide

There is a National Helpline for survivors of bereavement through suicide.

Tel: 0844 561 6855, 9 am to 9 pm every day

Timebank

A national charity providing volunteers with information on voluntary work and volunteering projects in the UK.

Tel: 0845 456 1668

Website: www.timebank.org

Scottish Partnership Agency for Palliative and Cancer Care

Website: www.palliativecarescotland.org.uk

World Health Organisation

WHO is the directing and coordinating authority for health within the United Nations system.

Website: www.who.int/en

CHAPTER 8

SUPPORT

At some time in our lives, most of us will have to support someone who is either caring for someone at the end of life or someone who is grieving or in mourning for a close friend or relative. This can be a most challenging time however much we desire to help our friends or family, and many find it difficult to know what to do or say.

It is the feeling of being powerless in the face of so much emotional pain that seems to strike a chord in many people. They want to reach out and help and yet feel impotent when they look for a way to do so. Indeed, they may feel so helpless and awkward that they react by avoiding the person they most wish to help.

When my son was at nursery school one of the other mothers there, whom I knew only slightly, had a miscarriage and word got around as these things do. I felt really sorry for her as I knew she had been delighted about the pregnancy, but I didn't know what to say or do. I wasn't sure whether she would want it mentioned and I didn't know if she would think our acquaintance so slight that if I said anything it might seem intrusive. For several days I just passed her by with the usual 'Hello', and then it seemed too late to say anything. To this day I regret not saying I was sorry.

Suppose we are in a situation where someone says, 'Am I dying?' The worst (and very common) response of 'Don't be silly; you will be fine' benefits no one. The person who asks that question needs to talk, and your avoidance will further isolate them at a time when they already feel cut off from the world. It may not be your job to say 'Yes', but you can ask, 'What have you been told?'

Someone who is ill may say, 'I don't know anything; no one is talking to me.' You could perhaps say, 'I will try to find a doctor who will explain what is happening to you.'

If someone tells you, 'The doctor says I am dying,' your replying 'That must have been a terrible shock,' or 'I am so sorry' may sound trite but these are empathetic responses that allow the person concerned to carry the conversation further if they wish.

It can be very difficult coping with questions or remarks that are 'unanswerable' such as:

'Why did this happen to me?'

'It's not fair.'

'What did I do to deserve this?'

There is no need to feel that you should have the answers. The questions are rhetorical and the questioner is almost certainly not expecting an answer; what they are perhaps looking for is someone just to listen. It is far more empathetic to say that you wish you knew or that you agree that life is unfair than find platitudes that heal no one. You can say:

'I wish I knew the answers,'

'I wish I knew how to help you,' or

'I don't understand it myself.'

Anything is better than avoidance and changing the subject.

In my role as a Crisis volunteer I had a conversation with a 74-year-old man who had been living on the streets for 14 years, since he lost his job as the doorman of a fancy London hotel. During the course of quite a long conversation he told me that he was thinking of jumping in front of a train. 'This isn't a life that is worth living,' he said to me, 'is it?' I was faced with say-ing, 'Well, it could be worse,' or 'I'm sure it will get better,' and for one split second I was tempted to do that, but I stopped, realising that for him it couldn't be much worse and it would not get better. So I said, 'I can certainly see why you would feel like that.' He touched my arm briefly and said, 'Thank you for not lying to me, and thank you for listening. It has been wonderful to be able to tell one person how I am really feeling.' It would have been much easier to say, 'Don't be silly, I'm sure you will get housing soon,' but I knew he wouldn't because he refused to be placed in a hostel – the first step to housing – because he couldn't bear the people he would have to be living with.

Many people find it very difficult to phone or approach someone who has recently been bereaved, and often put off contacting them. As time passes they feel more and more awkward until it seems too late, and then they are uncomfortable because they haven't called. Some-times due to this embarrassment the whole relationship breaks down. People find themselves diving into the nearest shop or toilet or under the nearest counter to avoid a face-to-face meeting with someone who they know is grieving or has had a diagnosis of a terminal illness.

So what can we say when we don't know what to say?

Sometimes the most sincere statement of all is simply to say, 'I heard about xxxx and I don't know what to say.' Or even simply, 'I really don't know what to say.' It is easy to relate to a straightforward state-ment like this. It shows that you care enough to want to say something. It allows the person you are addressing to follow up in the way they choose. Or you could say any of the following:

'I am very sorry to hear about xxxx.'

'I am so sorry. This must be a very difficult/painful time for you.'

'I heard about xxxx. I can't imagine how you feel.'

There are some things it is better not to say. For example, do not say (even if you think it) 'It was for the best'.

Other things to avoid saying are:

'It's horrid to be so incapacitated. I'm sure he wouldn't want to have lived like that.'

'Her time had come.'

In the immediate aftermath of death it is very difficult for those who are left to think rationally that death might be preferable to life with some incapacity or injury. The bereaved person wants the dead person back *at any price*. It is only much later that sometimes one may begin to believe that death might have been preferable to a lifetime of supported living or that a quick unexpected death might be considered to be better than a protracted and painful one. Even when the person who has died was suffering from a severe physical or mental incapacity or perhaps had dementia and their life didn't seem worthwhile to those looking on, it does not mean that the bereaved family do not feel sad at the death. None of us can judge the worth of another person's life (although sometimes it seems that health professionals try to do so) and none of us can understand the true depth of another person's grief.

Try not to say:

'I know how you feel.'

'He/she has had a good innings.'

'You will get over it.'

'At least he/she didn't suffer.'

When my granddaughter died suddenly at the age of six one of my co-workers came up to me and said, 'My grandmother died last year, so I know how you feel.' I felt like slapping her! How could she compare the death of an older woman with the death of a child!

However, even if you find yourself inadvertently blurting out something like these statements, don't rush away in embarrassment or feel guilty about your blunder. At least you have had the courage to approach the subject. If you feel you have said the wrong thing you can add, 'I'm so sorry. That was a stupid thing to say.'

Sometimes we hear that someone has been given bad news about their life coming to an end, or that someone close to a friend has died and we are not in a position to meet them and talk. It can be just as difficult to pick up the telephone and speak as to meet face to face. However, the kind of statements listed above can all be said on the telephone.

> *When my husband died my former boss telephoned. He was a very straightforward man, but I could tell he had psyched himself up to say the 'right thing'. He said, 'I'm so sorry to hear about John.' And I said quickly, 'Thank you. I'm really better if I don't talk about it.' He didn't mind this. He understood and the ice had been broken on the subject.*

If you do not know someone very well and you feel awkward about phoning them, you can always write to them. It used to be considered 'not the done thing' to send a sympathy card after a death (a letter was the correct thing) but these days cards are acceptable. Indeed, most people who have been bereaved are very glad to receive any token of sympathy. Sometimes the sheer number of cards and letters received is a great comfort.

If you are writing a card or a letter, then try to say something personal. People who have been bereaved usually really want to hear and see the name of the person who has died. It is nice to write a couple of sentences about the past such as, 'We always remember our lovely holidays together when the children were small,' or 'Alan had such a great sense of humour.' Even simple statements such as, 'I will always remember Peter with great affection,' are very comforting.

For someone nearing the end of life, knowing that people are sorry and will miss you can also be comforting. Cards which carry 'thinking of you' messages and short hand-written notes that carry sincere wishes are usually very acceptable. Do not send 'get well soon' cards to someone who knows that they are dying. Personal visits are usually welcomed but, of course, always check first with the carer that a visit will not be too tiring or come at an inappropriate time.

When someone has died, those closest to them will be in a state of shock. They may find it very difficult to respond even to sympathetic queries or expressions of condolence. It is good to understand this and not to take offence if our well-meant expressions of sympathy are not met with polite replies. The first days after someone has died are usually very busy for those left behind. At this time the best way to support them is to offer practical help. Don't say, 'If there is anything I can do to help just ask,' unless you mean it. Be sincere, and it is also better to be specific in your offers. Remember someone who has just been bereaved will find it hard to organise even day-to-day things.

It is better to say something along the lines of:

'Would you like me to take the children out for an hour?'

'I'd be happy to do some shopping for you.'

'Shall I post those letters for you?'

'I could help organise the funeral tea if you would like.'

Be specific if you want to help someone. A vague 'If I can do anything' or 'I'm here any time you need a shoulder' may make the speaker feel virtuous, but the receiver of such platitudes may feel that they are polite but insincere words and will most likely reply with, 'Thanks, but I'm fine at the moment.'

The first weeks after the funeral can be a very difficult time for the bereaved. Often it is still too early for them to be able to talk much about their feelings. However, there is sometimes a strong urge to repeat again and again the events leading up to death – to re-live them almost. If you wish to support someone at this time then allow them this form of self-therapy. Do not be quick to jump in and say things like:

'You don't want to talk about that now.'

'You'll only upset yourself.'

Instead, keep your remarks neutral. For example, you could say, 'It must have been very upsetting,' and do not hurry to point out that you have heard the story before.

You may be able to help at this time by offering invitations for quiet non-taxing outings and by being there when the bereaved person wishes for company. There is a common feeling that you should not leave a bereaved person alone in these early days, but everyone is different.

> *When my wife died, all my family came to support me and I was glad to have that. But sometimes I really felt the need just to sit quietly and think. One day I was reduced to going and sitting out in the garage so that I could get a few moments alone. It was a place no one thought to look for me.*

By all means be there for someone but listen to what their reaction is telling you. It is better to say, 'Would you like to go out for lunch/dinner/coffee next week. I'm free on Monday or Wednesday,' (which gives the grieving person the opportunity of saying either, 'Thanks, I'll let you know' if they are not yet ready for company, or 'Thanks, Monday would be great,' if they are), than to say, 'Come on, you really can't sit here feeling sad all the time. You have to face the world,' or something similar. In a world where, thanks to electronic communications, people are constantly busy and 'on call', perhaps the best offering in the way of our support is our uninterrupted time and attention.

> *After my husband died the only way I could get through the first days after the funeral was to know I had a planned activity for the next day when I went to bed each night. The activities weren't major outings or events: sometimes it was lunch with a friend, sometimes it was just clearing out a cupboard or going to the garden centre to buy some plants. Just having something 'time-tabled' helped me get on with life.*

It is very important to stay in touch and give on-going support. Don't make assumptions based on how the person looks from the outside. Some people are very good at hiding their feelings and the fact that they look fine doesn't mean that that is how they feel. Saying, 'You look well,' or 'You are so strong,' may put pressure on someone to continue to hide their feelings. If you see that someone wants to cry or is crying, perhaps just sit with them and allow them to cry without saying or doing anything to stop the flow of tears. Tears are healing and crying is a normal and healthy reaction. We sometimes feel that we should 'do something' when someone is crying. If we really want to help, a very caring look or a gentle and loving touch is the best thing we can do. It is worth remembering, however, that not everyone wishes to show their deepest feelings in public. You sometimes hear people say, unthinkingly, things like:

'She won't get over it until she lets herself cry.'

'She still hasn't cried, and that's a bad thing.'

There is no way to know if someone has been crying in private or if someone needs to cry at all. Crying is an understood sign of grief and upset, but not everyone needs to reveal their feelings in this way.

Someone who has to return to their job shortly after bereavement faces a compounded difficulty. Not only do they have to deal with the awkwardness in their home environment but also with a difficult return to the workplace. Many complain that they are greeted with a wall of silence by their co-workers, who don't know what to say and as mentioned above are scared of saying the 'wrong thing' and so say nothing at all. In addition to this, the symptoms of grief, most especially the difficulty in making decisions, forgetfulness and lack of concentration are quite contrary to 'normal' workplace behaviour.

Men and women's reactions to grief in the workplace are different. Women may agonise over how to ease the female co-worker's return. 'Should we say something, or should we pretend nothing has happened?' or 'How can we get over the initial awkwardness?' Meanwhile, the bereaved person is likely to be dreading the first day, wondering if they can cope with what people say (or do not say). Men, on the other hand, don't generally have this concern; they either say nothing or just say, 'Sorry to hear your news, mate,' with relatively little thought or preparation for the event.

> *I was a practice nurse in a doctors' surgery at the time my little girl was killed in a car accident. I dreaded returning to work, although I also was desperate to get back into 'normal' life. For-tunately for me, the Senior Partner telephoned me at home and suggested I drop into the staff room for coffee. They didn't lay on anything special for me but most of the staff dropped by and it was easy to get the preliminaries over because everyone was busy and most could only stay a few minutes. When I started back to work the following week everything was a lot easier.*

It is thoughtful to have a card saying 'welcome back' or flowers and so on, if someone has been off work for an extended period. However, work colleagues should be prepared for such gestures to provoke tears and it is kind to give people some privacy if this happens. Showing continued interest in their well-being and remembering that after a few weeks it is more than likely that their co-worker will be feeling worse and not better, is a good way of giving support.

If you have experienced a loss yourself and feel that you can help, then try saying something along the lines of, 'I don't know how you feel. I just know that when I lost XXX I found it so hard to come back to work/I was glad to be back amongst my friends.'

For managers, giving the employee a reasonable amount of flexibil-ity in both working hours and time off is a considerate gesture. This can help them cope with the combined stress of work and grief and shows that you understand that the grief process takes time and that the worker cannot 'snap out of it'.

A manager could perhaps say:

'I am very sorry to hear of your loss. How can we best support you?'

'Please let me know if I can help in any way.'

'If there is any way the company can support you through this, please tell me.'

'I can lighten your workload for XXXX period of time, if you feel that will be helpful to you.'

If a bereaved female employee is tearful, passing a tissue or asking her if she wants to be excused for a few minutes is quite acceptable. If appropriate, either she or her associates (especially if they are female) can make a joke about buying shares in waterproof mascara, or say "Thank God for waterproof mascara!' which can lighten the atmosphere without causing offence.

I worked as a support worker for a major charity and I really thought I would not be able to cope with returning to work after I had nursed my mother through a long illness and dealt with her death. But I can honestly say that my work saved my sanity. It gave me a reason to get up each day, a fixed routine and dealing with other people's problems gave me something other than my own feelings to think about.

I always take the example of two ladies whom I knew well. They grew up in the same neighbourhood and both met and married their childhood sweethearts and had two children. Their husbands worked in the same factory and they spent much of their leisure time together. Both husbands died in their early 70s within a few weeks of each other. One of the women died of a broken heart within a year of her husband, the other blew their life savings on a cruise and remarried within a year of her husband's death. Neither of these women could have said to each other, 'I know how you feel' when their husbands died. No one knows how anyone else is feeling – ever.

It should never be assumed that someone is not grieving just because they had a very troubled marriage or relationship with the person who died. Often the death of a partner in a troubled relationship can lead to a difficult grieving process.

> *When my ex-husband died I felt very sad and tearful but what made it a lot more difficult to grieve was the attitude of my friends who gave me no support at all, believing that, because our relationship had been quite stormy and our divorce full of recriminations, I would not grieve. I was surprised at how sad I felt when he died. I had spent a large chunk of my life with that man and in spite of it all had a very strong attachment to him.*

Perhaps the bereaved still has unsettled arguments raging in his or her head, but no one to direct these arguments at. Contradictory feelings and emotions are not easily laid to rest. People are also often grieving for the good relationship they either lost or did not have. Their grief is complicated by the fact that they will not now ever be able to 'make peace'. They may feel immensely guilty that they were not able to give the person who has died the right support at the end of life.

In trying to support bereaved friends or relatives in this position it is best to avoid saying things such as:

'But you never loved him anyway.'

'You wouldn't have been able to resolve your differences even if she had lived.'

'Don't feel guilty. He wouldn't have.'

In the early months after a bereavement people may find they forget things easily, tire more easily and find it harder to do the things that were done before almost without thinking. Decision-making may be very difficult, particularly if about matters where, for example the deceased partner in a relationship would have made the decisions before.

In many relationships one partner makes most of the decisions about finances, for example. It may also be very difficult to make decisions alone for people used always to discussing and making decisions together. If you want to help in this situation you can encourage the breaking down of the decision-making process into smaller components and talk things through without, of course, actually making decisions for the bereaved person. As an example, suppose the bereaved person is trying to organise a holiday with his/her children. He/she may have said something like, 'I know I should take the children away. They need the break and so do I. But XXX always used to decide where we were going and book everything.'

You could begin by asking, 'Would you like to holiday in this country or abroad?' In this way you could help the person you are supporting to come by easy stages to deciding what they wish to do. If you wanted to help further you could offer to go with them to make the booking or help them to search for a holiday cottage on the internet. Be careful not to slip into the role of decision-maker for them, however, unless this is a role you wish to assume.

As time goes by the tendency is for those around the bereaved to start to think that they are 'getting over it'. To a certain extent of course they will be coming to terms with what has happened and learning to adapt to the absence of the dead person, but in fact we never 'get over' a calamitous event in our lives. The events in our past shape our future and our present character. So you should try not to fall into the trap of thinking that because some months have gone by the bereaved person doesn't feel the need to talk about the deceased.

There was a particular woman at work who meant well. I think she might have been told in the past that people who have been bereaved should be allowed to talk. But whenever I brought up my dead husband's name I sensed her embarrassment. Often I wasn't saying anything special. If you have lived with someone for 30 years most of your experiences include them and their

> *name comes out naturally when you relate stories. I know this*
> *woman meant well, but each time his name came out she would*
> *visibly go into 'sympathetic listening' mode.*

Anniversaries

Anniversaries are hard after bereavement and unless we know the grieving person very well we may not know what those anniversaries are. Of
course there is the first Christmas, the birthday of the deceased, the
wedding anniversary, but what do we as supporting friends or family
know about the small occasions in the life of every relationship which
are between those in the relationship? What about the fact that your
mother used to buy you a bar of chocolate every Saturday? Or that your
father would always send a joking email on the anniversary of the day
you passed your driving test? Or that you and your husband used to
go to a church service together every Good Friday? Or that your son
always came into the bedroom early on Sunday with a cup of tea? If a
bereaved friend is unusually tearful on a day that doesn't seem special,
it may be worth keeping in mind that for them the day may have been
'special' in the past.

Some times are always harder than others. Christmas is a family
occasion for many and may be especially difficult for many years after
bereavement. Invitations around this time are likely to be very welcome. If you ask someone to a family Christmas meal though, think
carefully beforehand. It can be hard to be part of a different family on
this day and not know their customs and 'in jokes'. Allow the recently
bereaved some quiet time if they seem to want it and don't feel you
must 'jolly them along'. You could perhaps ask them to bring along an
item of food or organise some part of the proceedings. Maybe this is
the year to make a change to your 'traditional Christmas'?

The first anniversary of a death is difficult. If your friend or relative
wants to visit the grave, say a prayer in church, or drink a toast to the
one who has died, do not dismiss this as 'morbid'. It will help if you

give your support, perhaps offer to go with them to church or the grave-side or buy the champagne!

> *A friend said casually, 'Of course you have all those anniver-saries to get through' as though this was a 'set piece' grieving process. I think she meant well but it really upset me. Was my grief just a set of anniversaries to get through? After I'd 'been through' them would everything be different?*

There is another tendency on the part of well-meaning friends and relatives and this is thinking that once the first anniversary of a death is over everything will be back to 'normal'.

> *Actually one of the hardest times for me was the first few weeks after the first anniversary of my wife's death. Unconsciously I suppose I had thought that after this anniversary everything would be different. When I came to the realisation that it wasn't – that I still missed her just the same – I became very depressed.*

Another assumption often made is that a different person can act as a 'replacement' for the one who has died. You hear of doctors telling couples who have just lost a child that they 'have plenty of time to have another baby'. Sometimes people say carelessly, 'She's young enough to marry again' of a young widow. People also often refer to 'lucky' circumstances such as 'She's lucky that her son is still living at home.' Or perhaps, 'Luckily they have two other children.' It may be a comfort for a widow to have a son living at home but this will not replace her dead husband. In the same way, no new baby will replace the child that has died, although again, a new life may bring some comfort.

Well-meaning people also often think about trying to arrange a new partner for someone who has been bereaved. Our world is still based on couples and even numbers. Chicken pieces and lamb chops are sold in pairs, people invite equal numbers of men and women to a party, invitations are often sent to someone '… and partner' and parents with two children are considered a more complete family than parents with one child. Some people do find it very difficult to live alone and will marry or begin a new partnership quite quickly following the death of a spouse, but for others the healing period needs to be much longer. It is best to try to be sensitive here and not to rush to make obvious introductions unless you are sure they are welcome. Another way to be supportive is to allow someone who has been bereaved and is 'alone' sometimes to join you and your family on outings or special occasions without feeling that you or they have to hunt around for a 'partner' to be there with them. It really is not so very difficult to have a meal out with three or five people rather than four or six. If you are planning a trip to the theatre or cinema with your partner then why not invite the bereaved person along sometimes? If you are throwing a barbecue, then you don't have to invite people in couples. A natural acceptance of someone's new single status can make a huge difference to them.

Although all my women friends were kind and supportive after my husband died, they only invited me out to 'girls' events'. None of them invited me out with her husband or with another couple and I was no longer included in group events like concert visits where people attended in couples. I think it was kindly meant really but I did begin to feel a bit of an 'oddity'.

After my seven-year-old son died from a brain tumour, people stopped inviting us out as a family. My daughter missed being invited to parties on occasions when she and her brother would have gone together. Although I often didn't feel like going out, my daughter needed the company and I felt really upset on her behalf.

Support

There is a letter from an anonymous nurse that was quoted in Ward *et al*'s *The Art of Dying* in 1992 and first appeared in the *American Journal of Nursing* in 1970. (E. Seravalli suggests that doctors and nurses are often adversely affected by death, either because they themselves fear death and identify with the dying person or because they feel professionally impotent in the face of it.) Perhaps it is optimistic to believe that we have all moved on from the lonely position from which she speaks, but her message is a universal one and so we have included the letter in its entirety:

'I am a student nurse. I am dying. I write this to you who are, and will become nurses, in the hope that by sharing my feelings with you, you may someday be better able to help those who share my experience.

'I am out of the hospital now – perhaps for a month, for six months, perhaps for a year – but no one likes to talk much about such things. In fact, no one likes to talk about much at all.

'Nursing must be advancing, but I wish it would hurry. We're taught not to be overly cheery now, to omit the "everything's fine" routine and we have done pretty well. But now one is left in a lonely silent void. With the protective "fine, fine" gone, the staff are left with only their own vulnerability and fear. The dying patient is not yet seen as a person and thus cannot be communicated with as such. He or she is a symbol of what every human fears and what we each know, at least academically, that we too must someday face. What did they say in psychiatric nursing about meeting pathology with pathology to the detriment of both patient and nurse? And there was a lot about knowing one's own feelings before you could help another with his. How true.

'But for me, fear is today and dying is now. You slip in and out of my room, give me medication and check my blood pressure. Is it

because I am a student nurse, myself or just a human being, that I sense your fright? And your fears enhance mine. Why are you afraid? I am the one who is dying!

'I know, you feel insecure, don't know what to say, don't know what to do. But please believe me, if you care you can't go wrong. Just admit that you care. That is really for what we search. We may ask for whys and wherefores, but we don't really expect answers. Don't run away... wait... all I want to know is that there will be someone to hold my hand when I need it. I am afraid. Death may get to be a routine to you, but it is new to me. You may not see me as unique, but I have never died before. To me, once is pretty unique.

'You whisper about my youth, but when one is dying, is he really so young anymore? I have lots I wish we could talk about. It really wouldn't take much more of your time because you are in here quite a bit anyway. If only we could be honest and both admit our fears, touch one another. If you really care would you lose so much of your professionalism if you even cried with me? Just person to person? Then it might not be so hard to die – in a hospital – with friends close by.'

Quoted with the permission of *The American Journal of Nursing* (*1970*)

If we were to sum up how to support someone who is either grieving or at the end of their life, perhaps these words of the anonymous nurse say it all: 'But please believe me, if you care you can't go wrong. Just admit that you care. That is really for what we search....'

Further sources of help and information

The Samaritans
This listening service is available to those in emotional distress.
Tel: 08457 90 90 90
Website: www.samaritans.org

Winston's Wish
Offers practical support and guidance to families, professionals and anyone concerned about a grieving child.
Tel: 08452 030405
Website: www.winstonswish.org.uk

Cruse
A bereavement charity that has branches all over the country. Free confidential help to bereaved people.
Tel: 0844 477 9400
Website: www.crusebereavementcare.org.uk

CHAPTER 9

LEGACIES AND MEMORIALS

The information in this chapter is relevant for those who are nearing the end of life and wish to arrange their own legacies or memorials. It is also for those who may be planning a memorial after someone else has died. Most of us want to be remembered, and leaving a legacy or planning a memorial before death is one way of trying to perpetuate that memory. Considering arranging a memorial can be a very important and active part of coming to terms with the death of someone close to us.

A 'legacy' is money or possessions or anything else which is handed down or handed on to a successor. The term is usually applied to leaving possessions in a Will. A memorial is something set up, built or displayed to preserve the memory of someone (usually after death). A legacy can be used to create a memorial and money can be left 'in memoriam' or 'to the memory of' a person.

Most people consider whether they wish to leave a legacy when writing a Will, but if you are approaching the end of life, you may wish to consider or reconsider what you are leaving and to whom. Occasionally people make promises such as: 'When I die, you can have my silver-backed hairbrushes,' but unless these wishes are written down the legacies may never be made. The executors of a Will may not know of these verbal promises and they may not be able to fulfill them. There are actually strict rules about what an executor can and cannot do with the possessions left behind by someone who has died, and although not everyone adheres to these rules it cannot be assumed that a verbal promise will be kept. There are occasions where families can agree amicably on the dispersal of minor possessions, but this is not always the case. It is best to make sure that legacies are set down in a properly signed and witnessed Will.

My grandmother always used to show me a dress ring that I admired and say, 'This will be yours after I am gone.' However, I was not in the country when she died and I do not know what was in the Will. My grandmother's eldest son dealt with everything after her death and I never heard about the ring, which upset me. It wasn't the money value (I don't think it was worth anything really) so much as the keepsake value. I only returned to this country a couple of years later and I felt it would be indelicate to start asking questions about her possessions.

My mum didn't want to favour any of her six children and her 'estate' was left to us equally. However, in her last few years she used to show us a glass biscuit barrel on the sideboard and tell us if we fancied any small value item we should write it down on a piece of paper and put this in the biscuit barrel. She never did anything formal about this, but we all knew about it. Amazingly when she died we discovered that no two people had asked for the same thing and so we each got something small to remember her by. I don't know how legal this was but we certainly didn't argue amongst ourselves about it!

You can leave a monetary legacy to create a lasting memorial and this will be discussed later in the chapter.

Not everyone feels the need to think about legacies in advance. Some consider that those left behind can arrange things. You often hear the phrase, 'You can't take it with you'. However, the act of making a Will (see chapter 1) is one of the most important and most thoughtful things that you can do for those you are leaving behind.

Nearly 75 per cent of people in the United Kingdom donate money to charities during their lifetime, but fewer than 5 per cent leave money to charities after their deaths. As Paul Farthing, director of legacy fundraising at Cancer Research UK, points out, just one in seven actually leave a gift to charity in their Will, yet one in three say they'd consider it.

Leaving a legacy to charity is an excellent way to make your generosity last beyond your lifetime. If you decide to make a charity a beneficiary you'll need to know the full name and registered charity number. You can find these details at www.rememberacharity.org.uk (see further information below).

Our Samaritans branch was recently left a legacy, which was very helpful. The running costs of the branch are astronomical and that is without factoring in the constant need to recruit new volunteers. The legacy also allowed us to buy a new computer – the old one was always crashing – and we had enough left over to buy comfortable chairs for the volunteers. It made a big difference as sometimes our volunteers are on duty for five hours at a time.

Basingstoke Branch of Samaritans

Not everyone nearing the end of life is interested in planning their own memorial. Often those who have children see them and any grandchildren as a truly lasting memorial. Some people think it either morbid or unnecessarily egotistical to think about such things. However, it is rare for there to be no memorial at all after someone has died. Most people left behind feel the need for something – a gravestone, a memorial plaque, an entry in a book of remembrance at the crematorium or graveyard. Many also want to have some other lasting form of remembrance and get great comfort from planning and executing a memorial.

The style of memorial you may want is, of course, a very personal decision so it is important to take time to think about what would best reflect the personality, interests or the beliefs of the person who has died. It may not be advisable to make your choice when you are still suffering from shock and are in deep distress, although the decision to plan the memorial is often made then. A memorial project is something that can also be a joint decision and a proposal that would be good to talk over with family and friends. There are many different and wide-ranging ways to remember someone that you love and many original forms that this can take, as well as some more traditional ones.

Memorial stones and plaques

If you decide to have a memorial stone, make sure you select a memorial mason who specialises in what you are after and who belongs to the National Association of Memorial Masons (NAMM) or the British Register of Accredited Memorial Masons (BRAMM) or an equivalent body if you live outside the UK. It is also worth considering whether you should choose a small, independent firm or part of a larger company. The mason should understand stone and so be able to give you reliable advice as to whether the material you want to select is suitable for the type of memorial you are choosing and the area where it is to be placed. Different weather conditions and surrounding vegetation all have an effect on the stone and expert advice is needed. Memorial stones can be very expensive and some people object to the large amount being deducted from their 'legacy'. It is worth remembering, though, that the cost of a memorial stone can be deducted from the value of the estate before valuing it for inheritance tax purposes.

If you are planning a gravestone on the site after a burial this is a long-term project because gravestones cannot normally be erected for several months after the burial. The ground has to settle first. However, this may give the chance to hold a second memorial ceremony and some people find this is a comfort since a funeral has normally to be arranged in haste.

The scattering of ashes can be a memorable occasion. In some crematoria the ashes can be buried in an urn with a memorial stone. Others will allow a memorial plaque on a special wall, perhaps in a memorial garden. The individual crematorium will be able to advise what their protocols are, but whatever you choose there will be a cost involved. Some churches may have a memorial garden where they allow the scattering or burial of ashes and/or the erection of a plaque in memory of the deceased. Some crematoria and some churches have a 'book of remembrance' where names can be inscribed. Where this is done the pages of the book are normally turned each day so that relatives and friends can call in on anniversaries to view the memorial to their own loved one. For those who have lost someone and are looking for a more contemporary, individual or unique memorial, there are artists who specialise in different memorials individually ordered, and these can be designed in a way that may reflect the personality of the deceased individual.

In many cases, plans are made to scatter the ashes at a later date, perhaps in a place that holds special significance or happy memories for the deceased or the family. This can also be an occasion for a second memorial ceremony and sometimes (as in erecting a memorial stone) the planning of this can be a comfort in the weeks after the funeral. Customs and rules differ in different places, but generally the crematorium will hold the ashes for a limited time (there is sometimes a fee for this) whilst plans are made for collecting and scattering them. Most funeral directors will also take care of the ashes until you are ready to collect them if you agree this with them when you make the funeral arrangements. As mentioned above, scattering the ashes or erecting a memorial stone or plaque can both be good occasions to hold a second memorial ceremony or life celebration. Sometimes the later date allows relatives or friends who were unable to attend the funeral to pay their respects and the lapse of time after the death means that this ceremony, although it may still be very poignant, is not so emotional as a funeral inevitably is. This occasion may be much more relaxed and more comforting for those who were very close to the deceased since they can consider any prayers, readings, songs or valedictory in a calmer frame of mind than at the time of arranging a funeral.

We had originally planned to scatter my wife's ashes rather quietly in a wood where she had walked often with our dogs. However, when they heard the plan, quite a few relatives who had not been able to get to the funeral asked if they could come along. My daughter wanted to bring her children along and my son brought his girlfriend. It turned into a bit of a party and I was happy to think that my wife would have loved it.

Early one morning I took my mum's ashes out into her garden, which she had loved and tended right to the end. I dug a small hole and buried them. I remember it was rather a misty morning on a damp autumn day and I wouldn't say the occasion was uplifting. But I wanted to do this alone and I wanted Mum to be where she had spent many happy days. I felt closer to Mum at that moment than I had at the funeral.

Memorial services

In the past, memorial services were only held for the famous or for those who for some reason or another could not have a normal funeral (such as those lost at sea). There is an increasing demand for memorial services now, possibly because of the feeling that justice has not been done to the memory of the deceased due to the need to arrange funerals swiftly. If you feel this then a memorial service might be an appropriate idea. Such a service or ceremony need not necessarily be religious in nature and could simply be a family and friends get-together at home, in a place that has significance for the deceased, or in somewhere like a local hotel or hall which is accessible to as many people as possible. The occasion can be semi-formal, with readings or eulogies and a period of silence to remember the deceased, or it can be more relaxed. One suggestion is to have pictures of the deceased displayed and perhaps a 'memorial board' where people can write their own remembrances or good wishes. Music which was loved by the deceased can be played and a toast drunk to their memory.

Many religions and cultures have a day in the year when the dead are especially remembered. In the Christian religion this tends to be on 2 November, which is All Souls Day, and some parish churches hold a special service around this time at which a candle is lit in memory of all those parishioners who have died during the past year. Churches which hold this tradition will usually notify anyone with whom they have had contact about the date of the ceremony, but if you have not been invited then it is simple to ring the office of the local church and enquire if such a service is happening. Roman Catholic churches have a tradition of having a mass said 'for the repose of the soul' of someone who has died. Even if you do not hold religious beliefs you are usually welcome at these services and many find them consoling and reassuring.

> *We always have a Mass said for our deceased parents on a Sunday near to their birthdays. Each of us takes it in turn to arrange this at their local church and afterwards we meet for a meal and some of us who have travelled furthest stay overnight nearby. It makes a family occasion and means that we always remember Mum and Dad in a particularly happy way.*

Charitable donations

It is very common these days to find a request for 'No flowers – donations to XXX' on funeral notices. Often people feel that it is more beneficial for mourners to give the money which they might have spent on flowers to a good cause and frequently a charity is chosen in which the deceased had an interest. Just as often charitable donations are requested to go to an organisation or charity that has helped the deceased and their family in the past, perhaps in the months leading up to the end of life. For example, if the deceased had some form of cancer, donations to cancer research are often requested. For many charities 'in memoriam' donations form a major part of their income. Arranging an easy way for mourners to make a donation to charity instead of buying a funeral wreath or flowers is an excellent way of helping others at no cost to oneself.

Sometimes those who have been bereaved may wish to do more.

> *We were so impressed with the care that my mother-in-law received in her nursing home that we gave them a gift of £3000 out of our inheritance. The home asked us if we wanted the money spent on anything in particular. It seemed that we could have asked them to buy a certain piece of equipment or furniture if we had wanted. However, we told them to use the money where they felt it would do the most good. The matron said that ideally she would employ an extra carer but that wasn't possible with this amount. I believe they bought some garden benches with the money so that residents could sit outside on sunny days.*

There are a few ways to leave money to a charity. You can make an outright bequest and this is always acceptable. If the bequest is coming out of the deceased person's estate then a donation to charity may qualify for inheritance tax relief. Some charities will allow you to specify the use to which you want the money put; for example, you may want the gift to go towards a particular piece of research. This is not always possible though.

If you received help from the local branch of a national charity and wish any gift to go specifically to that branch you would be wise to ask beforehand how you can ensure that this happens. Sometimes cheques made out to a national charity go into a central fund and the money may not reach the branch concerned. Some charities operate in such a way that local branches have to do their own fundraising and operate their own accounts and you would need to ensure that any cheque was gifted to the actual branch where you wished the money to go. (This will also apply if you are asking for gifts to the local branch of a charity instead of floral tributes.)

There is significant benefit when considering leaving a legacy or donating money to charity on someone's behalf. Some organisations really make a difference in the world and they rely on donations in order to be able to do this. You can help them to make that difference. Some people have always supported a cause by either giving donations or actively participating, but others perhaps need to think about a cause they or the person they wish to commemorate supported and find a charity that represents this cause.

Most national and international charities have made it as easy as possible for someone to donate. Electronic donations can often be made via a web page or, if this is not so, a web page will certainly indicate how you can most easily make the donation. A simple telephone call will also get you information about how to make a donation. If you are a tax payer you will probably be able to 'gift aid' your donation, thereby allowing the charity to receive even more money.

Perhaps you wish to give something tangible to a local charity rather than a gift of money. It is always best to ask the organisation concerned beforehand about such a gift. It would be a shame to donate a piece of furniture say, which could not be used because it did not fit health and safety criteria, or to give equipment with which the charity was already well endowed. You might feel that the person in whose memory you are making the donation would like you to make a specific gift but a discussion with the people 'on the coal face' might result in your gift being much more useful and appreciated because it is really needed.

Often people have the idea that they would like to set up a charity in the name of the person who has died. Many splendid charitable organisations have been started in this way. However, before you decide to adopt this idea take the time thoroughly to investigate whether there is already in existence a charity which fulfils the role you envisage. There are many charities which seem to have the same aims as other charities and dissemination of donations may actually mean that less is being done by a larger number of organisations. If there is already a charity which supports your cause and you feel that a simple donation is not enough then perhaps you can give money to open a local branch, to help build a much needed facility or to fund a particular line of research. A new branch, a new building or a research fund could be named for the person you wish to commemorate. The first thing to do is to approach the charity in question and explain what you would like. Any charity will be open to a discussion about donations like this.

If you really wish to set up a new charity you will need proper legal advice, a business plan and plenty of time and energy. This is not something which can be arranged easily and you will want to take advice from the Charities Commission. There are quite strict rules governing registered charities. For example, a registered charity must be set up for the 'public benefit' – this means an organisation's activities benefit a sufficient section of the community and not just a few selected people. It may be that when you investigate further you will find that your aims do not fit the criteria, but you may be able to fulfill your wishes in a simpler way.

> *In memory of my partner who died suddenly and unexpectedly I wanted to set up a charity which would help struggling young musicians to remain true to their art and which would 'assist, mentor and educate musicians to further themselves, both in writing and promotional terms, to inspire and to aspire'. Originally I was planning to set up a registered charity but after taking advice from the Charities Commission I set up a trust which aims to financially assist needy musicians and bands where it's needed most, at grassroots. My partner never stopped moving forward musically and I feel the Trust reflects his life and aims.*

When my granddaughter died I was determined to make sure she had a memorial that would be a real tribute to who she was. With my daughter's permission I paid for a new children's playground to be built near her house and in the middle of the playground I commissioned a small sculpture of a young girl in a ballerina pose with her name and dates underneath. The playground soon became known by my granddaughter's name and I spend many hours sitting on one of the benches watching the children play and remembering her. More than once I have witnessed a child looking at the sculpture, and I have been able to tell them who it represents and a little about my beloved granddaughter. It has given me a place to go when I have wanted to grieve quietly and a feeling that her short life has not been forgotten.

Material memorials

Providing a material memorial can be a way to share and celebrate your memories. What will be central for you will be to make the memorial significant, and for it to be meaningful it needs to reflect some aspects of either the personality, beliefs or life of the person that you want to remember. Someone who loved pets may want some money to go towards giving pets a better home or a charity that reflects the love of animals. Someone who cared deeply about education may like to sponsor a bursary at a university. Someone who loved and appreciated art may be best remembered by having a picture painted in his or her memory or a sculpture that would in some way mirror a memory of the person. Although there are some commonly accepted ways of creating a memorial there is no limit to the possibilities. Here are some of the most usual and some of the more unusual ideas for preserving a memory.

Many of us are familiar with the concept of the wooden seat or bench with a plate inscribed, for example, 'In memory of XXX who loved this place'. Many local councils will allow the dedication of a bench in a local park or amenity site. Generally you will pay for the bench and a small inscribed plaque will be fixed on it. Some councils will allow you to 'adopt' a bench which they have already provided. The Woodland Trust will set up a bench with an inscribed plaque in natural woodland in return for a set donation. Some people think that they can just have a bench made and set it down wherever they like, perhaps beside a favourite pathway. However, by doing this you run the risk of having your bench removed and wasting your money. There are no standard rules concerning the dedication and provision of benches 'in memoriam' and you will need to contact whoever owns the land where you would like the bench to go. Some places have strict rules about who can and who cannot be remembered with a bench dedication. Of course there is nothing to prevent you having a memorial bench made and placed in your garden or own land.

> *My husband and I used to walk along the river at least once a week for over 40 years and when he died my daughter paid for a bench with his name on it to be placed on the river bank near the tree where he proposed to me all those years ago. It has been wonderful for me to sit there and remember those years – and more than once I have had the feeling that he was sitting there right next to me.*

New buildings are frequently dedicated to the memory of someone who may have been connected either with the building or with the organisation involved in the use of the building. If you think that this would be a fitting memorial to someone who has recently died you should approach the organisation concerned.

> *Our local scout group had raised the money to build a new headquarters. Whilst it was still being built one of most dedicated fundraisers was killed in a serious accident. It was decided to name the building after him.*

Locomotives have names and many a train enthusiast would love to have a train named after them. Locomotives' names are decided upon informally by individual companies without any official process and anyone can apply to have a train named as a memorial, although most railway companies would expect there to have been some significant connection with the company before they would agree to this.

An unusual idea which is actually gaining in popularity is to have a small portion of cremated ashes turned into a permanent memento, such as a glass object or jewellery. It is possible to extract the carbon from the ashes under extreme heat to turn into a lasting object.

I wanted a visual record of our life together after my partner died but I didn't want it to have 'sad' overtones. In the end I made a dramatic collage using photographs, letters and pieces of material and buttons from some of his favourite clothes plus a couple of small keepsakes. When it was framed it not only gave me the memorial I wanted but made a striking visual focus in my hallway.

If you or someone else close to the deceased are gifted in the creative arts then the composition of a piece of music, a poem or the dedication of a book or play is a different and lasting memorial and the composition can also be very cathartic as part of the grieving process.

When my friend, who was a locally well-known singer, died unexpectedly, we wanted to create a memorial to him. We had been part way through writing an album and had recorded some demos ourselves. We took those recordings to a studio, which helped us to turn the demos into a releasable product while maintaining our friend's originally recorded parts, allowing us to finish what he had started. The proceeds from the sale of this album went to

> *help young emerging musicians in our local area. It really helped*
> *us to come to terms with his death and look to the future.*

Plants as memorials

There are many ways to use plants to remember someone who has died.
For example, you can dedicate anything from a whole stretch of woodland to one tree through an organisation such as The Woodland Trust
or you can pay for trees to be planted in a forest in Israel, for example.
However, what most of us will be familiar with is the planting of a bush
or shrub (rose-bushes are frequently chosen because of their scent and
their variety of names), in honour of someone's memory.

> *My mother was living in sheltered housing. After she died a rose*
> *bush was planted in her memory in a special garden, which was*
> *kept for the purpose of remembering everyone who had lived*
> *and died there. It is a beautiful, well-kept garden. I don't often*
> *go back there but it is wonderful to think that not only is my*
> *mother remembered but so are all the other late residents and*
> *that they are remembered in a way that can give so much pleas-*
> *ure to those still living.*

One of the benefits of choosing a plant is that it becomes a living memorial. There are an enormous number of plants with names (not just
rose bushes) and many good nurseries and garden centres will have a
facility to look up these names and help you choose something that will
match the memory you wish to mark. Another way to use plants for this
purpose is to choose a plant that will flower around the birthday of the
person who has died or perhaps around the anniversary of their death.
Alternatively, you could choose a plant which the deceased especially
loved or one in their favourite colour.

> *I have bought and planted a different shrub or tree for everyone I want to remember. For my father I have an azalea, which always flowers around his birthday. For my mother I have chrysanthemums because they were her favourite flowers. To remember my father-in-law I have planted a clematis, which bears his christian name, and for my mother-in-law I transplanted from her garden a small tree which she cared for very much. After my husband died I decided to buy a lemon tree because he was very fond of the taste of lemon.*

> *When my mother died unexpectedly at the age of 45 one of her friends sent me a certificate showing that she had planted 20 trees in my mother's name in Israel. My mother was Trinidadian and a Rastafarian by religion, but I knew she would have deeply appreciated this gesture, as did I.*

Actions and activities as memorials

Some people would prefer to use actions and activities as a form of memorial. For example, a popular action is to run a marathon or do one of the various charity walks (such as Race for Life – Cancer Research UK; Memory Walk – Alzheimer's Society) which are often run as annual events. Sometimes those who wish to mark their remembrance in a special way will undertake a sponsored event in the name of the person who has died, afterwards donating the proceeds to a suitable charity. Often walks or sponsored events are used as a fundraiser towards a material memorial, such as much-needed equipment for a hospital or a special garden attached to a care centre.

Notice of death in a newspaper or trade journal is fairly common, but this method is increasingly being used to remember someone on an anniversary or to announce a memorial service or action due to be taken as a memorial. Some journals will accept memorial notices free of charge and you may find that you receive some welcome follow-up in the form of contacts or condolences from past acquaintances.

Online tributes are a more modern expression of testimonial. There are websites which specialise in online memorials or you can create your own website. Family and friends can add their memories to the site. Children can also participate in this and add their own thoughts, memories and perhaps poems. Online memorials have the advantage of being easily accessed by everyone who wants to add their thoughts and of being inexpensive or in some cases completely free. There are often specific sites already in existence as a tribute to those who died in particular circumstances or as a result of certain events, and if this applies to the person you wish to remember than adding their name and a tribute on the website may make a fitting memorial to the person you loved.

Further sources of help and information

Battersea Dogs' and Cats' Home
Tel: 020 7622 3626
Website: www.battersea.org.uk

Justgiving
A company which aims to enable any charity, however small, to use the web to raise money at very low cost.
Various telephone numbers – see website
Website:www.justgiving.com

Remember a charity
Works to encourage more people to consider leaving a gift to a charity in their Will.
Tel: 020 7840 1030
Website:www.rememberacharity.org.uk/find_a_charity.jsp

Memorials by individual artists
Tel: 01728 688934
Website: www.memorialsbyartists.co.uk

Jewish National Fund
Planting trees in the Holy Land.
Various local office telephone numbers – see website
Website: www.jnftrees.com

The Forward4Wiz Trust
The trust exists to provide advice and support to bands and individual
artists.
Website: www.f4wt.org

Appendix one

Example: *My End-of-Life Wishes*

I would like to be buried
I would like to be cremated
I would like my ashes to be scattered on
I would like a   funeral
The flowers I would like are
I would prefer to be buried in/near
The music I would like played is
The hymns I would like sung are
The poem I would like to be recited is
I would like everyone to wear
My favourite colour is
I would like   to write the eulogy
I would like the wake to be at
The drink I would like to be served is
The food I would like to be served is

End of Life

I would particularly like   to attend
I would like to be remembered for
I would like to be dressed in
I would prefer my casket be made of
My Will is kept at
The money I have put aside to pay for this is in

Appendix two

Helpful organisations and websites listed in the book

INDEX

Index

About the authors

Mary Jordan works for a national dementia charity and is an Associate Director of ELM (End of Life Management Ltd). She has had considerable experience of caring for elderly relatives and friends and worked in the NHS for 9 years. Earlier publications include books on Caring and on GP Practice Management, in addition to articles in nursing and social care journals and magazines.

Judy Carole Kauffmann was a hospice volunteer and passed an Open University Course in Death, Dying and Bereavement after which she became a carer/companion to a lady with dementia and then the Registered Manager of a Domiciliary Care Agency in Hampshire. She is passionate about caring for people during their end of life journey and empathising with those left behind, and her training in all areas of social care and her writings reflect this ethos. Judy is the Managing Director of ELManagement Ltd who offer training in all aspects of social care and is an associate trainer with Age UK (formerly Age Concern) as well as an associate trainer with a leading dementia specialist training company.

For more information about their work go to:
www.endoflifebook.com
www.ELManagement.org